delicious soups

fresh and hearty soups for every occasion

Belinda Williams

photography by Steve Painter

RYLAND PETERS & SMALL
LONDON • NEW YORK

Design, photography and prop styling
Steve Painter

Editor Rebecca Woods

Production Gary Hayes

Art Director Leslie Harrington

Editorial Director Julia Charles

Food stylist Lucy McKelvie

Food stylist's assistant Ellie Jarvis

Indexer Hilary Bird

First published in 2013 by
Ryland Peters & Small
20–21 Jockey's Fields
London WC1R 4BW
and
519 Broadway, 5th Floor
New York, NY 10012

www.rylandpeters.com

10 9 8 7 6 5 4 3

Text © Belinda Williams 2013
Design and photographs © Ryland Peters
& Small 2013

Printed in China

UK ISBN: 978-1-84975-438-5
US ISBN: 978-1-84975-463-7

A CIP record for this book is available from
the British Library.
US Library of Congress CIP data has been
applied for.

Notes
• All spoon measurements are level unless
otherwise specified.
• All vegetables are medium-sized unless
otherwise specified.
• All eggs are medium (UK) or large (US),
unless otherwise specified. Uncooked or
partially cooked eggs should not be served
to the very old, frail, young children,
pregnant women or those with
compromised immune systems.
• When a recipe calls for the grated zest
of citrus fruit, buy unwaxed fruit and wash
well before using. If you can only find
treated fruit, scrub well in warm soapy
water before using.
• Ovens should be preheated to the
specified temperatures. We recommend
using an oven thermometer. If using a
fan-assisted oven, adjust temperatures
according to the manufacturer's
instructions.

contents

introduction

Love, health and humour: the three most important things in life and the three most defining elements in this book. Everyone knows that home-cooked food is good for you – good for the soul, good for the heart and good, in most cases, for the waistline! Soup is the food of endless versatility, comfort and joy.

It is because of the simplicity of soup, and its relevance to just about any culture or occasion, that we decided to start our company producing homemade soup on a commercial scale – and thus Yorkshire Provender was born. I am proud of my heritage and wanted to bring the farmers and food producers to the fore, and to create a tangible link between producer and consumer, so often void on our supermarket shelves. A hand-crafted product produced by real people with real stories who care passionately about what they do. We remain one of the few soup producers who use fresh vegetables from sources we know. Our relationships with our growers and farming roots are still at the core of our ethos and guide us in all we do.

Happily, just about anyone can make soup, regardless of culinary ability. Simply start with quality ingredients, treat them well and the result will be delicious! I am very visually led and often seek inspiration from a single vegetable: a perfect cabbage, tender baby spinach or a gnarly celeriac/celery root – they all lure me in and beg me to turn them into something wonderful.

I hope that I can encourage you, through the recipes in this book, to explore the endless possibilities of this wonderful medium. I have included all manner of options, from rustic fish stews to elegant veloutés with scallops, so there is truly something for every occasion.

Whether it be a picnic on the beach (try the Fresh Spinach Soup with Minted Pea and Coriander on page 56), a cosy lunch around the kitchen table (try Scottish Root Vegetable Soup with Pearl Barley and Thyme – see page 126), or a formal dinner party starter and show stealer (try shooters of Beetroot and Parsnip Soup with Horseradish on page 64, with a smoked trout and wasabi salad), a soup can be applied to all occasions, and it will do its job brilliantly. Like the perfect cashmere sweater, soup can be dressed up or dressed down and, regardless of the company, is always effortlessly appropriate.

I would also hope that you make each soup your own. If you are missing an ingredient or want to substitute one vegetable for another, then do – it will be different, but it will not be a failure! I am the daughter of wartime babies and my parents were, and still are, from a generation who believed in throwing nothing away! I have that hangover from my childhood, where leftovers were half the fun of meal times. My mother would make bubble and squeak with leftover cabbage and mash, and meatballs with leftover Sunday joint passed through a huge hand-turned mincer/grinder clamped to the kitchen table. I still get an excited, satisfying pleasure in creating meals out of whatever I find left in the fridge, and much like my mother's, mine is always crammed full. Soups cry out for leftovers to be used, and most soups can be adapted to suit what you have left.

It is my memories of great experiences, moments, people and places that have inspired the recipes in this book. I hope you enjoy making these soups, and have the confidence to create some new ones of your own.

stocks

In this book I have referred to 'stock'. I would never insist you make your own as there are some good powdered or compound stocks available (although try and use one with as few artificial additives as possible or your delicious soup could end up tasting like a poor packeted relation!). But I would actively encourage you to take the time to make your own. You can make these when you have a little time available or appropriate ingredients to hand and pop them in the freezer.

vegetable stock

2 onions, halved

2 leek, thickly sliced

1 fennel bulb, halved

4 celery sticks, thickly sliced

4 carrots, peeled and thickly sliced

1–2 bay leaves

a few sprigs of fresh thyme

a small bunch of fresh parsley

10 white peppercorns

sea salt

makes about 1.5 litres/6 cups

Put all ingredients in a large saucepan and top up with 2.5 litres/quarts water. Cover the pan with a lid, bring the liquid to a simmer. Let it simmer for 1½ hours, removing the lid for the last 30 minutes so it can reduce a little. Pass the stock through a sieve/strainer and discard the solids. Adjust the seasoning with salt and use as per the recipe.

Tip: If you prefer a slightly richer flavour, brown the vegetables in a tablespoon butter before adding the liquid to the pan.

fish stock

50 g/3½ tablespoons butter

2 garlic cloves

12 shallots, peeled

1 leek, thickly sliced

2 kg/4½ lbs. white fish carcass/bones (not oily fish or salmon), heads and all but no guts

4 celery sticks, thickly sliced

½ fennel bulb, halved

2 carrots, peeled and thickly sliced

a large bunch of fresh tarragon

a large bunch of fresh parsley

10 peppercorns

sea salt

makes about 1.5 litres/6 cups

Melt the butter in a large saucepan and add the garlic, shallots and leek. Cook for a few minutes until softened, then add fish to the pan. Top up with 2 litres/quarts water. Add the celery, fennel, carrots, herbs and peppercorns, cover with the lid and simmer very gently for about an hour, removing the lid for the last 20 minutes so that it can reduce a little. Pass the stock through a sieve/strainer and discard the solids. Adjust the seasoning with salt and use as per the recipe.

beef stock

3 kg/6½ lbs. beef bones

2 carrots, peeled and thickly sliced

1 onion, halved

3 celery sticks, thickly sliced

2 leeks, thickly sliced

1 bay leaf

a large bunch of fresh parsley

a few sprigs of fresh thyme

10 black peppercorns

sea salt

makes about 1 litre/4 cups

Preheat the oven to 200°C (400°F) Gas 6.

Put the beef bones in a roasting pan and roast them in the preheated oven for about 30 minutes to give colour and depth of flavour. Transfer the bones to a stock pan. Deglaze the roasting pan by pouring a little hot water into the pan to pick up any juices that are stuck to the pan (so no flavour is left behind!), then pour into the stock pan with the bones. Add all vegetables, herbs and seasonings to the pan and top with 4 litres/quarts water. Cover the pan with a lid and bring to a simmer. Let simmer very slowly for hours and hours – the more the better and no less than 5 hours! Pass the stock through a sieve/strainer and discard the solids. Transfer the stock to a clean pan, return to the heat and cook, uncovered, until reduced to 1 litre/4 cups – this will intensify the stock's flavour. Adjust the seasoning with salt, and use as per the recipe.

Tip: Ask the butcher for marrow bones, as these will give the best jellied result. You know you have a good stock if it sets hard when cooled!

chicken stock

25 g/2 tablespoons butter or vegetable or olive oil

4 kg/8 ¾ lbs. chicken wings or a chicken carcass

2 onions, halved

1 leek, thickly sliced

2 garlic cloves

2 celery sticks, thickly sliced

200 g/7 oz. button mushrooms, halved

2 carrots, peeled and thickly sliced

a mix of fresh herbs, such as bay leaves, tarragon, parsley, chervil, thyme (for a very plain stock, use parsley only)

20 black peppercorns

sea salt

makes about 1.5 litres/6 cups

Heat the butter or oil in a large saucepan and add the chicken. Cook for a few minutes in the butter, without colouring, then add the onion, leek and garlic and cook until softened. Add all other vegetables to the pan and pour over 3 litres/quarts water. Add the fresh herbs and the peppercorns, cover the pan and bring to a simmer. Let the stock simmer for 1½ hours, removing the lid for the last 30 minutes so that it can reduce a little. Pass the stock through a fine-mesh sieve/strainer and discard the solids. Skim the stock, if necessary. Adjust the seasoning with salt, and use as per the recipe.

hearty & wholesome

chunky provençal vegetable soup with smoked paprika

This is such a simple and quick soup, and you can use up little left-over bits of vegetable, as only small amounts of each are needed. The quantities and ingredients below are a rough guide because really you can use whatever you happen to have in your fridge. The smoked paprika and balsamic bring it together to give a great balance of interest on the palate.

50 ml/3½ tablespoons olive oil

1 red onion, diced

2 garlic cloves, crushed

½ courgette/zucchini, diced

1 carrot, peeled and diced

2 celery sticks, sliced

1 small leek, white only, sliced

800 ml/3⅓ cups vegetable stock

a 400-g/14-oz. can chopped tomatoes

50 g/3½ tablespoons tomato purée/paste

a good pinch of smoked paprika

200 g/7 oz. mixed canned butter/lima beans and kidney beans, drained

a small handful of green beans, sliced into short lengths

1 tablespoon balsamic vinegar

a small bunch of fresh basil, roughly chopped

a small bunch of fresh parsley, roughly chopped

sea salt and ground black pepper

serves 6–8

Put the olive oil, onion, garlic, courgette/zucchini, carrot, celery and leek in a large saucepan and toss over medium heat for about 3–4 minutes, until they have taken up the oil.

Pour in the stock and chopped tomatoes, then add the green beans and tomato purée/paste and stir everything together. Simmer for about 15–20 minutes, until the vegetables are tender.

Add the smoked paprika, mixed beans and balsamic vinegar to the pan, cooking for a minute to heat the beans through. Season to taste with salt and black pepper and stir everything together. Finally, stir in the freshly chopped basil and parsley, reserving a little to garnish.

Ladle the soup into chunky rustic bowls and serve scattered with the reserved fresh herbs.

green summer soup

This soup is inspired by sitting in the garden of my dreams and creating a soup with a little bit of most things I find there! The base needs soft vegetables that are happy to be puréed, but any green vegetable can be added, as long as they are not too tough. Throw them in right at the end so that they are simply blanched. The cream is optional – you may prefer this with none, but frankly, I am a bit of a glutton and love my dairy. Alternatively, use crème fraîche, if you prefer. As you will...

Melt the butter in a large saucepan and add the onion, potato, celery and leek. Cook for a few minutes, until beginning to soften, then pour over the stock. Bring the liquid to a simmer and cook for about 15–20 minutes, until the vegetables are tender. Add the courgette/zucchini, beans, peas and herbs to the soup, bring it back to a simmer and cook for 2–3 minutes, then add the spinach and rocket/arugula and draw off heat. Blend the soup with a stick blender until smooth, then season with salt and pepper. Stir in the cream, if using, ladle the soup into bowls and serve.

75 g/5 tablespoons butter

1 onion, diced

1 potato, peeled and diced

4 celery sticks, sliced

1 leek, white only, sliced

1.5 litres/6 cups vegetable or chicken stock

2 courgettes/zucchini, diced

200 g/1½ cups skinned, fresh baby broad/fava beans

250 g/1¾ cups fresh baby peas

leaves from 2 sprigs of fresh tarragon, chopped

a bunch of fresh chervil, chopped

a large bunch of baby spinach

a bunch of rocket/arugula

200 ml/¾ cup cream (optional)

sea salt and ground black pepper

serves 6

gently spiced vegetable soup with chicken, coconut and ginger

Some 25 years ago, I found myself sitting in a beach café on the island of Ko Samui in Thailand. The weather was perfect and the view magnificent. This was the dish of the day for lunch, but it was deliciously elegant and had enough attitude to make it interesting and let the freshness of the lime and coconut sing out. I made it my mission to get straight in the kitchen when I got back to the UK to recreate this lovely broth. I think this is pretty close!

2 tablespoons light vegetable oil

1 garlic clove, crushed

a 3-cm/1¼-inch piece of fresh ginger, grated

1 red chilli, finely chopped

6–7 spring onions/scallions, finely sliced and whites and greens separated

1 red pepper, deseeded and finely sliced

1 green pepper, deseeded and finely sliced

4 carrots, peeled and very finely sliced

2 celery sticks, very finely sliced

300 ml/1¼ cups coconut milk

750 ml/3 cups vegetable stock

1 tablespoon tomato purée/paste

500 g/1 lb. cooked chicken

a squeeze of lime juice

a splash of fish sauce

a handful of fresh coriander/cilantro, chopped

a small handful of sugar snap peas, sliced lengthways

sea salt and ground black pepper

chilli oil and lime wedges, to serve (optional)

serves 6

Put the oil in a large saucepan set over high heat. Throw in the garlic, ginger, chilli and spring onion/scallion whites. Toss around the pan for a few seconds, then add the red and green peppers, carrots and celery to the pan, followed by the coconut milk and stock. Stir in the tomato purée/paste and add the cooked chicken, then pop the lid on the pan and simmer for a few minutes, until the vegetables are wilted and the chicken is heated through. Season to taste, adding a squeeze of lime juice, a splash of fish sauce and the chopped coriander/cilantro.

Just before you are ready to serve, throw in the sugar snap peas and the sliced spring onion/scallion greens. Ladle the soup into bowls and serve drizzled with a little chilli oil, and with lime wedges on the side, if wished.

yorkshire ale, caramelized onion and thyme soup

I have had a charmed life, not least being spoilt by the pleasure of local English pubs serving traditional Yorkshire bitter. My great friend Eddy Theakston comes from a long line of great brewers. He remains in the family business and was thrilled when I asked him if I could use his Best Bitter to make my 'take' on a French onion soup (which would normally use an Alpine white wine). This soup has now been adopted by numerous soup makers and is on the menu in many a local pub. It's buttery and sweet, with the bitter balance of a good old Yorkshire ale.

40 g/3 tablespoons butter

3 large onions, finely sliced

2 large garlic cloves, crushed

20 g/2 tablespoons dark muscovado/dark brown sugar

200 ml/¾ cup ale

800 ml/3⅓ cups beef stock

2 tablespoons Dijon mustard

3 sprigs of fresh thyme

a handful of fresh parsley, chopped

sea salt and ground black pepper

for the roux (optional)

30 g/2 tablespoons butter

1 tablespoon plain/all-purpose flour

to serve

6 slices of baguette

olive oil, for brushing

grated Gruyère cheese, or other strong hard cheese

serves 6

Melt the butter in a heavy-based saucepan, add the finely sliced onions and cook over gentle heat until very soft and reduced in volume. They need to be silky, and with no resistance at all – this will take about 20–25 minutes. Add the garlic and brown sugar and cook for a few more minutes to allow the onions to take on a deep golden colour, but do not let them crisp.

Pour over the ale and stock, then add the mustard and fresh thyme. If your thyme is of the 'stalky' variety, pick off as many of the little leaves as possible, but add the stalks to impart their flavour, which can be pulled out before you serve. If you are using soft summer thyme, roughly chop and add it all. Simmer for about 10 minutes to allow all the flavours to infuse. By this time, the onions should be as soft as butter and have no resistance to the bite.

To thicken the soup a little, make a roux. Gently melt the butter in a small saucepan, then remove the pan from the heat and stir in the flour. A little at a time, add the roux mixture to the simmering soup, stirring all the time to prevent lumps. This will gradually thicken the soup just enough for it to be slightly syrupy. (It is not a thick soup, but the roux adds texture and makes it slightly more hearty. If you are cooking for someone who doesn't eat wheat, it can be left out altogether.) Season the soup with salt and plenty of freshly ground black pepper, then stir in the freshly chopped parsley.

Preheat the oven to 180°C (350°F) Gas 4. Brush the baguette slices with a little olive oil and bake until golden brown.

Ladle the soup into heatproof bowls, place a slice of the baked bread on top and scatter with a generous amount of Gruyère. Place under a hot grill/broiler to melt the cheese, then serve.

hearty soup of root vegetables with ground beef

This is my take on 'Mince and Tatties' – a mainstay warming lunch when the weather outside is cold and your time is short. It can be cooked ahead of time and left in the fridge for up to four days, and will only get better. If you don't have minced/ground beef, you can use lamb instead and add a little rosemary. Equally, if you have some meat left from the Sunday joint, you can mince/grind or roughly chop it up and use that instead. If you prefer some of the vegetables to others, or have more of one type available than another, just make up to the correct volume with your own choices. It's a great way to use up leftovers!

2–3 tablespoons vegetable oil

250 g/9 oz. minced/ground beef

1 small onion, diced

2 large garlic cloves, crushed

½ swede/rutabaga, peeled and diced

1 small carrot, peeled and diced

½ celeriac/celery root, peeled and diced

2 celery sticks, sliced

1 small leek, white only, sliced

1 small potato, peeled and diced

a 400-g/14-oz. can chopped tomatoes

800 ml/3⅓ cups beef stock

60 g/4 generous tablespoons tomato purée/paste

250 g/1¼ cups frozen or fresh peas

a small bunch of fresh parsley, chopped, plus extra to garnish

a few sprigs of fresh thyme

a splash of Worcestershire sauce (optional)

sea salt and ground black pepper

serves 6

Melt the oil in a large heavy-based saucepan. Toss in the beef and fry until browned, stirring all the time to brown the meat. Add the onion and garlic and continue to cook until the onion is translucent and softened.

Add all the vegetables and stir them into the meat and onions, making sure there is no clumping of any one ingredient – you want them all evenly dispersed. Add the chopped tomatoes, beef stock and tomato purée/paste and put the lid on the pan. Allow to simmer gently for about 12 minutes, or until the vegetables are almost soft – you don't want them mushy, as a little 'al dente' (I think) adds to the eating experience. Now add the peas and herbs and season with salt and black pepper. If you want a little extra flavour, add a splash of Worcestershire sauce and simmer for a few more minutes to let all the flavours marry, before spooning into warmed bowls, to serve.

Tip: If you are not eating the soup immediately, the peas are better added just before the soup is required, so that they retain their lovely green colour. This soup is perfect served with delicious multi-grain bread and unsalted butter, but to make it into even more of a meal, you could also add lovely herby dumplings: serve one or two with each portion and scatter with plenty of fresh parsley.

maria's minestrone

A couple of years ago, I received a handwritten letter in a spider scrawl full of passion and personality. It was from one Maria Townsend, who talked of her love for our soup and her enthusiasm for a 'real' brand, and asked for the opportunity to meet us. It is so rare, these days, to receive a letter, not least a handwritten one, and it struck a chord with me. Maria has been my right hand now for two years and we have been on quite a journey during this time. Her passion is as fierce as ever, only matched by mine – we make quite a team! This is her minestrone – she loves it, so I am guessing you will, too.

2 tablespoons olive oil

4 rashers/slices of bacon, chopped

1 large onion, diced

3 carrots, peeled and diced

1 celery stick, sliced

1 leek, sliced

3 potatoes, peeled and diced

2 garlic cloves, crushed

a 400-g/14-oz. can chopped tomatoes

1.5 litres/6 cups vegetable stock

a handful (about 70 g/2½ oz.) of broken spaghetti, or similar

a 400-g/14-oz. can cannellini or haricot/navy beans, drained

250 g/9 oz. spinach or other greens, chopped

1–2 courgettes/zucchini, diced

a bunch of fresh parsley, chopped

1 teaspoon mixed dried herbs

paprika, to taste (optional)

sea salt and ground black pepper

freshly grated Parmesan cheese, to serve

serves 6

Heat the olive oil in a large saucepan and fry the bacon until browned. Add the onion, carrots, celery, leek and potatoes, put the lid on the pan and sweat for a few minutes over gentle heat, until the vegetables soften without colouring. Add the garlic to the pan and continue cooking for a few minutes before adding the chopped tomatoes, stock and pasta. Bring the liquid to the boil, then reduce to a simmer and cook until the vegetables are just tender and the pasta is almost cooked. Add the beans, greens, courgettes/zucchini and parsley to the pan and continue to cook for a few minutes until the greens are tender but still green. Season to taste with salt and pepper and, if you like a little heat, stir in a little paprika.

Serve generous portions of the soup in big flat bowls and finish with lots of freshly grated Parmesan.

puy lentil soup with seasonal greens and bacon

I came upon the inspiration for this wonderful rustic soup when a local farmer and my good friend, Peter Richardson, happened to give me the most beautiful savoy cabbage I have ever seen. I took it straight home and created this fabulous soup out of this magnificent vegetable! I use savoy cabbage, when in season, but sweetheart is also great, and of course wonderful spring greens when available – make it your own with whatever you love most. Use a nice big pan with a good heavy base to slowly cook and hold the heat evenly through the soup, and make sure all your vegetables are cut to about the same size so they cook evenly.

2–3 tablespoons olive oil

150 g/4 oz. bacon lardons or thick-cut dry cured bacon cut into matchsticks

1 small onion, chopped

4 garlic cloves, crushed

1 leek, sliced

1 celery stick, sliced

2 carrots, peeled and sliced

¼ celeriac/celery root, peeled and diced

¼ swede/rutabaga, peeled and diced

125 g/⅔ cup Puy lentils, rinsed and drained

1.3 litres/5½ cups vegetable stock

a 400-g/14-oz. can chopped tomatoes

1½ tablespoons tomato purée/paste

¼ small savoy cabbage or other greens (cut as a chiffonade, long and very fine)

a small handful of fresh parsley, chopped

a small handful of fresh thyme, chopped

sea salt and ground black pepper

serves 6–8

Put the olive oil in a large heavy-based saucepan, add the bacon, onion and garlic and cook until the onion is softened and the bacon is just cooked. Add the leek, celery, carrots, celeriac/celery root and swede/rutabaga to the pan, along with the Puy lentils. Stir to coat all the vegetables with the oil so that they absorb a little and glisten slightly, then pour over the stock and chopped tomatoes and season with salt and pepper. Put the lid on the pan and simmer very gently for about 15 minutes – you do not want a ferocious boil or the bacon will break up, and it is nice to have each element of this soup holding its own.

Draw the pan off the heat and stir in the tomato purée/paste, greens and chopped fresh herbs. Return to the heat and simmer until the greens are just tender but retain a little crunch.

Ladle the soup into rustic bowls, to serve.

300 g/10½ oz. chipolatas or other thin sausages

2 tablespoons olive oil

6 shallots, quartered

4 garlic cloves, sliced

100 g/3½ oz. Speck ham or thick-sliced back bacon, cut into large thick lardons

250 g/9 oz. butternut squash or other pumpkin or squash, diced

4 celery sticks, sliced

70 g/5 tablespoons tomato purée/paste

800 ml/3⅓ cups beef or chicken stock

a 400-g/14-oz. can chopped tomatoes

a good glug of red wine (optional)

a bouquet garni made up of fresh thyme, bay leaves and good few sprigs of fresh parsley

200 g/7 oz. mixed canned beans, such as haricot/navy or butter/lima beans (use whatever are your favourites), drained

a large handful of long French beans

a handful of fresh parsley, chopped

a handful of fresh thyme sprigs, leaves only

sea salt and ground black pepper

serves 6

cassoulet of chipolatas, beans and dry-cured ham

There is not much we Brits don't know about a good sausage, and the French cassoulet is an ideal platform to give the British banger its place. I like to use thin ones (herby chipolatas are especially good) that have been cooked under the grill/broiler or over an open fire, as the colour and caramelization of the skin adds to the dish and I love the slightly smoky flavour. Cut them on an angle and leave quite large, as this is supposed to be more of a stew than a soup, and all the ingredients need to be kept chunky and honest!

Cook the chipolatas under a grill/broiler until evenly browned. Leave to cool, then slice them on the angle into large chunks.

Put the oil in a heavy-based saucepan, throw in the shallots, garlic and ham and cook until all just beginning to brown, but do not over-colour. Add the squash, celery and tomato purée/paste then top up with the stock, tomatoes and wine, if using. Add the bouquet garni, put the lid on the pan and leave to simmer for 25 minutes. Add the canned beans, green beans and sausages and cook for another 3–4 minutes to heat through. Season with salt and black pepper, stir in the fresh herbs and serve.

red lentil soup with chicken, fresh turmeric, and chilli

This is ode to Jo Ropner, or otherwise known as 'super woman', who is a great friend and, among other things, a brilliant cook. After a lovely cycle one day, we refuelled our hungry hearts with a fresh turmeric and red lentil soup. This is an elaboration on hers – and is probably nowhere near as good! There is no doubt that if you can find the gnarly little stems of fresh turmeric they make this soup far superior. The root looks very much like slim ginger, but is, as you would expect, deep reddish orange in the centre. It has heat, but also an aromatic pungent flavour, and is a great addition if you can track it down. Dried turmeric is a good second best, so do try this soup anyway.

120 ml/½ cup ground nut or vegetable oil

4 boneless, skinless chicken breasts

2 onions, diced

2 carrots, peeled and diced

2 sweet potatoes, peeled and diced

a 5-cm/2-inch piece of fresh turmeric, grated (or 1 teaspoon ground turmeric)

1 red chilli, deseeded and very finely sliced

1–2 teaspoons red curry paste, to taste

4 garlic cloves, crushed

100 g/½ cup red lentils, rinsed

80 g/½ cup sultanas/golden raisins (optional)

2 litres/quarts chicken stock

sea salt and ground black pepper

leaves from a good bunch of fresh coriander/cilantro, to serve

Put the oil in large saucepan set over high heat and add the chicken breasts to the pan in a single layer. Cook for a couple of minutes, until browned, then turn them over and brown them on the other side. Reduce the temperature and cook for about 10 minutes until firm and cooked through, then remove the chicken from the pan and set aside.

Add the onions, carrots and sweet potatoes to the pan and cook over medium heat until just beginning to take colour, stirring occasionally. Add the turmeric, chilli (reserve a little, for the garnish), curry paste and garlic and cook, stirring, for a further minute.

Add the lentils, sultanas/golden raisins, if using, and stock to the pan and bring to a simmer. Put the lid on the pan and allow the soup to cook for 20 minutes or so, until the vegetables and lentils are tender.

Slice or roughly chop the chicken and add it back to the soup. Simmer for a further 10 minutes without the pan lid to reduce the liquid slightly and make the soup a little thicker. When all the ingredients have fused in colour and flavour and the sultanas/golden raisins are swollen, season to taste.

Ladle the soup into large bowls, garnish with the reserved chilli and fresh coriander/cilantro leaves, and serve.

serves 6–8

pea and ham soup with black pudding and butternut squash

This is a wonderful combination of drama and calm – the vivid simplicity of the green pea base dramatically contrasted with the black pudding and orange butternut pieces. My preference is to oven bake the black pudding to release as much fat as possible and achieve a lovely crisp outer. To add further sweetness and a touch of style, you could add a drizzle of reduced balsamic to serve.

100 g/7 tablespoons butter

2 onions or 6 shallots, finely diced

1 leek, sliced

1 potato, peeled and diced

1.8 litres/7½ cups chicken stock

500 g/3½ cups frozen or fresh peas

a few fresh mint leaves

150 g/5½ oz. cooked ham hock, shredded

200 g/¾ cup double/heavy cream

sea salt and ground black pepper

reduced balsamic vinegar, to serve (optional)

for the garnish

200 g/7 oz. black pudding, diced

200 g/1½ cups peeled, deseeded and diced butternut squash

olive oil, for drizzling

serves 6–8

To make the garnish, preheat the oven to 190°C (375°F) Gas 5.

Put the black pudding and butternut squash in a non-stick roasting pan, drizzle lightly with olive oil and toss to coat. Bake in the preheated oven for 15–20 minutes, turning at least once during cooking, until the squash is evenly golden and the black pudding is very dark (this will turn very black in the oven).

Meanwhile, start the soup. Melt the butter in a large saucepan and add the onions and leek. Cook for a few minutes to soften, then add the potato and stir to coat in the butter. Cover with the stock and simmer for 15–20 minutes, until the potato is tender. Add the peas and mint leaves and bring to the boil. As soon as the soup hits boiling point, draw the pan off heat and blend with a stick blender until smooth. Stir in the ham hock and cream and season with salt and black pepper.

Serve the soup garnished with the roasted black pudding and squash, and a drizzle of reduced balsamic vinegar, if wished.

mediterranean, aubergine, pepper and fennel soup with black olives and basil

The markets in the Mediterranean are an inspiration, and you can make this wonderful rustic soup by throwing together a bit of everything you might find on the vegetable stall... no fuss, no bother and whatever the weather! This soup is wonderful with a little croûton of fresh young goats' cheese served on top – just allow it to sit there for a moment before serving and see it melt around the outside. If you wanted to give the soup a cheffy look, you could serve it drizzled with reduced balsamic syrup and garnished with sprigs of tender thyme.

1 large aubergine/eggplant, chopped into 1-cm/½-inch thick slices, then in half again into half moons

1 large red onion, chopped into quarters, then quarters again

½ fennel bulb, cut into slim wedges

4 garlic cloves, whole and skin on

200 ml/¾ cup really good olive oil

2 courgettes/zucchini, roughly diced (but keep chunky)

2 red peppers

2 yellow peppers

6 ripe tomatoes, roughly chopped

600 ml/2½ cups passata (Italian sieved tomatoes)

500 ml/2 cups tomato juice or vegetable stock

a small handful of stoned/pitted black olives

a small bunch of fresh basil, chopped

sea salt and ground black pepper

sliced goats' cheese, to serve (optional)

serves 6

Preheat the oven to 200°C (400°F) Gas 6.

Put the aubergine/eggplant, red onion and fennel into a heavy roasting pan with the garlic cloves and drizzle with most of the olive oil. Roast in the preheated oven for about 15 minutes, until soft and slightly blackened, turning the vegetables once during cooking for an even colour. Towards the end of the cooking time, add the diced courgettes/zucchini to the pan and mix in with the other vegetables so that they cook for a few minutes and pick up a little colour and flavour.

Cut the peppers in half and remove the seeds. Lay them skin side up in a separate roasting pan and brush them with the remaining olive oil. Roast until the skin is beginning to blister – about 15 minutes (these can cook at the same time as the other vegetables). Leave to cool, then remove the skins and cut the peppers into strips.

Put all the roast vegetables (including any oil from the roasting pans) into a large saucepan. Squeeze the flesh out of the garlic cloves and add to the pan, discarding the skins. Add the chopped tomatoes and passata and cook over gentle heat, stirring, for about 20 minutes, until the passata has reduced and the vegetables have softened and are merging together. Add the tomato juice until a soupy but quite thick consistency is achieved (you may not need it all), then season with sea salt and black pepper. Finally, stir in the black olives and basil.

Ladle the soup into bowls and serve each topped with a slice of goats' cheese, if using.

spicy meatball soup with curly kale and roots

This wonderful hearty soup is a multicultural mix, with down-to-earth British veg, chilli from the equator and tomatoes from the Mediterranean. You can make your own meatballs with more, or less, of any of these influences as you like, or indeed use a really good sausage, cooked and sliced and added at the end – it's your choice. I have given a recipe for a simple pork meatball below, as it is very satisfying to know you made them yourself! Chard, kale or any cabbage can be used for this delicious wholesome dish.

3 tablespoons olive oil

4 small strong onions, diced

½ swede/rutabaga or turnip, peeled and diced

1 leek, white only, sliced

2 carrots, peeled and diced

2 parsnips, peeled and diced

2 red chillies, finely chopped

2 garlic cloves, finely chopped

400 ml/1⅔ cups passata (Italian sieved tomatoes)

1.3 litres/5½ cups vegetable stock

4 tablespoons tomato purée/paste

a good bunch of fresh thyme, leaves only, or tied into a bunch

150 g/¾ cup green lentils, rinsed

400 g/14 oz. meatballs (see tip)

a large bunch of curly kale, finely sliced

sea salt and ground black pepper

serves 6–8

Heat the oil in large saucepan, add the onions and cook for 3–4 minutes, until softened. Throw in the swede/rutabaga, leek, carrots and parsnips and toss around over medium heat for about 3–5 minutes. Add the chillies and garlic to the pan, then pour over the passata and stock and add the tomato purée/paste, thyme and lentils. Simmer the soup for 15 minutes, then add the meatballs carefully so that they do not get misshapen or stick together. Simmer for a further 10–15 minutes, until the meatballs are cooked through and firm. Add the kale and cook until it has reduced in volume and is tender. If you have added the thyme in a tied bunch, remove it now. Season the soup with salt and pepper, ladle into large rustic bowls and serve.

Tip: There are a few methods for making meatballs. A simple recipe is to combine 500 g/1 lb. minced/ground pork and 150 g/3⅓ cups breadcrumbs with a good amount of chopped fresh parsley and thyme, a crushed garlic clove and some seasoning. Bind it all together with an egg yolk and roll into walnut-sized balls. Alternatively, use a mix of pork and beef, or even chicken, but a bit of fat in the meatballs helps the soup. If you are feeling a little lazy, just squeeze the meat out of your chosen best sausage, and roll into nice-sized balls – damp hands will help these sticky little critters keep themselves to themselves! You could even use cooked sausages, sliced and added in at the end, if you prefer.

spiced lamb shank soup with redcurrant and rosemary

This is a two-stage process; first, you need to cook the lamb to impart the spice to the broth, which is then used to form the base for the soup. If you like a slightly thicker base to your soups, break up some chunky stale white bread and add this a few minutes before serving to thicken it in an authentic fashion.

Dry roast the cumin seeds in a frying pan for a couple of minutes to release their flavour, then set aside to cool.

Heat the oil in a large saucepan, add the lamb shanks and brown them over high heat. Add the onions, garlic, rosemary, spices and ginger and pour over the stock and red wine. Cover with the lid and simmer for 2 hours.

When the lamb is very tender, remove the shanks from the pan and set aside to cool. Strain the broth into a clean pan. If it looks at all fatty, allow to cool and skim well. Tear the lamb into nice generous pieces, but not too large to be too much of a mouthful.

Put the broth back over medium heat and add the carrots, celery, redcurrant jelly and lamb pieces. Bring the liquid to a simmer, then reduce the heat to low and gently cook until all the vegetables are tender – about 20 minutes. Remove the sprigs of rosemary and season with plenty of black pepper and a little salt. Add a squeeze of lemon juice to sharpen the flavour, if you wish.

Ladle the soup into bowls and serve garnished with extra sprigs of fresh rosemary.

1½ teaspoons cumin seeds

2 tablespoons olive oil

2 lamb shanks

2 large onions, roughly diced

2 garlic cloves, chopped

2 sprigs of fresh rosemary, plus extra sprigs to serve

1 cinnamon stick

4 green cardamom pods

a 5–7-cm/2–2¾-inch piece of fresh ginger, grated

1.5 litres/6 cups vegetable stock

½ bottle red wine

2 carrots, peeled and sliced

2 celery sticks, sliced

3 tablespoons redcurrant jelly

a squeeze of lemon juice (optional)

sea salt and ground black pepper

serves 6

chilli beef soup with corn frittas and guacamole

This is a great spicy little number, good for Bonfire Night or winter parties, or just a fun supper dish to liven up a week night!

2 tablespoons corn oil

2 red onions, chopped

400 g/14 oz. minced/ground beef

1 sweet potato, peeled and diced

½ butternut squash, peeled, deseeded and diced

1 red pepper, deseeded and diced

2 garlic cloves, chopped

1–2 red chillies, finely chopped

1–2 teaspoons ground cumin

a few sprigs of fresh oregano, leaves only, or 2 pinches of dried

2 tablespoons tomato purée/paste

900 ml/3¾ cups passata (Italian sieved tomatoes)

800 ml/3⅓ cups beef stock

2 x 400-g/14-oz. cans red kidney beans, drained

½–1 teaspoon sugar

dried chilli/hot pepper flakes, to taste (optional)

sea salt and ground black pepper

for the corn frittas

175 g/1½ cups polenta flour/fine cornmeal

100 g/1 cup grated Parmesan cheese

1 red chilli, finely chopped

a bunch of fresh parsley, chopped

75 g/5 tablespoons butter

sea salt

to serve

grated Manchego cheese

guacamole

a baking sheet, lined

serves 6–8

To make the corn frittas, put the polenta flour in a jug/pitcher so that you can pour it easily. Bring 1 litre/4 cups water to a simmer in a saucepan and add a little salt. Pour the polenta into the simmering water in a steady stream, stirring all the time. This will erupt and bubble, so stand back and be careful not to let it get too hot. Keep stirring until it is very smooth. The polenta is cooked when it falls away from the sides of the pan – this should take about 3–5 minutes. Stir in the Parmesan and chilli, then remove from the heat, season and stir in the parsley. Spread the polenta out on the prepared baking sheet to about 2 cm/¾ inch thick and leave to cool for at least 45 minutes. When cold and set, cut the polenta into small triangles. Heat the butter in a non-stick frying pan and fry the polenta evenly on both sides until crisp and brown. These can be set aside and reheated in the oven when needed.

To make the the soup, heat the oil in a large saucepan, add the onions and cook for a few minutes, until softened. Add the beef and cook for a further few minutes until browned, stirring all the time to break up the meat. Add all the vegetables to the pan, along with the garlic, chilli and cumin. Stir over the heat for a few more minutes, until all the ingredients begin to look a little cooked, then add the oregano, tomato purée/paste, passata and stock. Cover the pan and simmer gently for about 30 minutes. Towards the end of the cooking time, remove the pan lid and allow the soup to reduce a little as it is intended to be quite thick and hearty! Add the kidney beans and sugar and season to taste. If more heat is needed, add a few dried chilli/hot pepper flakes, to taste.

Serve the soup topped with the polenta croûtons and a good sprinkling of grated Manchego. A dollop of guacamole on top really enriches the soup and makes it a meal in itself.

british bouillabaisse

This is a play on the Mediterranean classic but without the fish heads and bones, which, I have to say, always rather get in the way of a good soup! This works amazingly well with any firm-fleshed white fish, so just use what you have – haddock, cod, monkfish, coral trout and red mullet would all work well. Make sure you use waxy potatoes and not floury ones as we want them to hold their shape and not break up in the soup.

50 g/3½ tablespoons salted butter

1 leek, white only, sliced

2 celery sticks (including leaves), sliced

1 large or 2 small waxy potatoes, peeled and diced

½ fennel bulb, finely sliced

½ yellow pepper, deseeded and diced

½ onion, diced

3 garlic cloves, crushed

a pinch of saffron fronds

a glass of fruity white wine (optional)

1.75 litres/7¼ cups fish stock

1 bay leaf

a small bunch of fresh thyme (if stalky, tie as a bunch and use as an infusion; if soft, chop the leaves and scatter into the soup)

400 g/14 oz. chunky white fish fillets

200 g/7 oz. raw shelled prawns/shrimp

400 g/14 oz. mussels, cleaned, bearded and ready to go

150 ml/⅔ cup double/heavy cream

a large bunch of fresh parsley, chopped

sea salt and ground white pepper

fresh crusty bread, to serve

serves 6

Melt the butter in a large saucepan set over medium–high heat and throw in all the vegetables along with the garlic and saffron fronds. Cook for a few minutes, stirring all the time, until the vegetables are softened, then add the white wine, (if using) and fish stock. Add the bay leaf and thyme and let simmer for about 15–20 minutes until the vegetables are almost tender.

Cut the fish into evenly-sized but interesting-shaped pieces and add to the pan with the vegetables, then add the shelled prawns/shrimp and mussels. Put a lid on the pan and allow to simmer for 3–5 minutes, until all the mussels have opened (remove any unopened shells). Stir in the cream and parsley, then season to taste.

Ladle the soup into large flat soup plates (you can remove the thyme stalks and bay leaves now if you do not wish to see these), and serve with plenty of fresh crusty bread.

I love smoked fish, and smoked haddock is something we do very well in the UK. Typically, the Scots use this in their 'Cullen Skink', which is one of the all-time classics. Natural oak-smoked haddock is delicate and delicious – and if you have access to a good smoker who uses the best oak chips, all the better.

Preheat the oven to 190°C (375°F) Gas 5.

Put the fish in a baking dish, and brush with 15 g/1 tablespoon of the butter, melted. Pour over the milk and cover the dish with a sheet of kitchen foil. Put the dish in the preheated oven and poach the fish for about 15 minutes, until it is just cooked and opaque. Pour off the poaching liquid, reserving it to add to the soup later. Remove the skin and debone the fish thoroughly by gently running a finger down the surface of the fish – you should feel the sharp little bones as you go – and pull out with your fingers or tweezers. Flake the fish into generous pieces, checking for bones as you go, and set aside.

Melt the remaining butter in a large saucepan and add the leek, onion and potato. Soften over gentle heat for a few minutes, then add the saffron and tumeric. Add the bay leaves and pour over the stock. Add the white rice and stir to prevent it sinking to the bottom. Simmer for about 12 minutes, stirring occasionally.

When the rice is tender, add the flaked fish to the chowder, along with its poaching liquid. Stir gently and add the cream, lemon zest and the lemon juice, to taste. Stir through the parsley, season well with black pepper and serve.

smoked haddock chowder

400 g/14 oz. smoked haddock

100 g/7 tablespoons butter

200 ml/¾ cup whole milk

1 leek, white only, sliced

1 large white onion, diced

1 large potato, peeled and diced

a good pinch of saffron fronds

a pinch of ground turmeric

2 bay leaves

750 ml/3 cups vegetable stock

100 g/generous ½ cup long-grain basmati rice

200 ml/¾ cup double/heavy cream

grated zest and freshly squeezed juice of 1 lemon

a bunch of fresh parsley, chopped

ground black pepper

serves 6

smooth & creamy

roasted tomato and garlic soup with oven-crisp parma ham and aubergine flatbread

This simple soup relies upon the best ingredients, so make sure you use really good olive oil as the flavour will come through. The flatbread is delicious without the soup, too – use it as a base for roast vegetables, top with mozzarella and pop in the oven for a rustic take on a quick pizza.

16 plum or large ripe tomatoes

2 red onions, cut into quarters

4 garlic cloves, whole and skin on

90 ml/6 tablespoons olive oil, plus extra to serve (optional)

6 tablespoons tomato purée/paste

about 1.5 litres/6 cups vegetable stock

sea salt and ground black pepper

for the aubergine and parma ham flatbread

2 aubergines/eggplants, diced

olive oil, for drizzling

5 garlic cloves, whole and skin on

6–8 flatbreads, tortilla or similar (not too thick)

8 slices of Parma ham or air-dried ham/prosciutto, cut into ribbons

a heavy roasting pan, lined with silicone paper or lightly greased kitchen foil

serves 6–8

Preheat the oven to 180°C (350°F) Gas 4.

Put the tomatoes, onions, garlic and olive oil in a bowl and toss together until evenly coated. Tip the vegetables into the prepared roasting pan and sprinkle well with sea salt. Roast in the preheated oven for about 25–30 minutes, until soft, caramelized and slightly brown (if they brown too fast they will not be soft and sweet enough). Remove the vegetables from the oven and turn the oven up to 200°C (400°F) Gas 6.

Pop the roasted garlic cloves from their skins and put them in the bowl of a food processor with the roasted tomatoes and onions. Add the tomato purée/paste and pulse until the mixture is smooth, then pour into a saucepan and add the stock gradually until you have a soup with a nice thick consistency. Heat gently to warm through and season with black pepper.

For the flatbread, put the diced aubergine/eggplant in a bowl, generously drizzle with olive oil and toss until well coated. Tip into a heavy roasting pan, add the garlic cloves and roast in the preheated oven for about 15 minutes, until soft and well coloured. Leave the oven on to bake the flatbreads.

Squeeze the garlic cloves out of their skins and put the flesh in the bowl of a food processor, along with the roasted aubergine/eggplant (reserve a few pieces to serve) and a good amount of sea salt. Pulse until almost smooth but retaining a little texture.

Spread the puréed aubergine/eggplant onto the flatbreads and scatter with the ham. Place the coated flatbreads directly onto the shelf/rack in the hot oven and bake for 10–15 minutes, until the ham is crisp and aubergine/eggplant topping sizzling. Cut the flatbreads into triangles, or as you like.

Ladle the soup into bowls (an extra drizzle of olive oil on top adds richness, if you wish), top with a few pieces of the reserved roasted aubergine/eggplant and serve with the hot flatbread.

fresh silky seasonal asparagus soup with sour cream and chives

Asparagus is a gardener's investment of time, but the result is worth every moment, as few vegetables can 'stand alone' in the kitchen the way asparagus can. Gardening was in my grandfather's blood and his asparagus patch was his pride and joy. So ode to Parker, my darling, inventive and ever-tolerant grandfather – this one's for you. This silky smooth, velvety soup is simple, elegant and perfect for any occasion. I like to serve it with a little sprinkle of chive flower petals, when you have them in your garden. The subtle purple mimic's the asparagus tips – so elegant, so delicious, so Parker!

50 g/3½ tablespoons butter

6 banana (or other sweet) shallots, diced

8 new potatoes, peeled and diced

1½ bunches of asparagus spears

800 ml/3⅓ cups vegetable or chicken stock

100 ml/7 tablespoons double/heavy cream and sour cream combined (for a little more 'edge' use all sour cream, or for a richer soup use all double/heavy cream)

sea salt and ground black pepper

freshly snipped chives, to serve

serves 4–6

Melt the butter in a large saucepan and add the shallots and potatoes. Toss them in the butter and cook very gently so that they take in some of the butter, but do not allow them to colour. Pour over the stock, cover and simmer for about 15 minutes, until the potatoes are tender.

Snap the woody ends off the asparagus spears. (Breaking them at the point at which they are naturally inclined to snap means you remove any woody, fibrous stalk, which is not good for the soup.) Roughly chop the spears and add them to the pan with the potatoes and stock. Cook for a few more minutes only, as we want to keep the vibrant green. When the asparagus is almost tender, draw the pan off the heat and blend the soup with a stick blender, adding the cream a little at a time as you blend, as this will help give the soup a silky finish. Season to taste with salt and freshly ground black pepper.

Ladle the soup into smart white bowls, garnish with freshly snipped chives and serve immediately.

purple sprouting broccoli soup with mrs bells blue

I like to use the purple sprouting variety of broccoli for making soup, when available, as the colour and flavour is superior and more intense. Mrs Bells Blue is a locally produced cheese by Shepherds Purse Cheeses, who use the milk from their own flock of sheep. Judy Bell has been a pioneer in cheese-making in the UK, and this soft blue cheese is one of her best. If it is unavailable, you can use any not-too-strong blue cheese as an option.

50 g/3½ tablespoons salted butter

6 banana shallots, finely chopped

3 potatoes, peeled and diced

4 celery sticks, sliced

1.5 litres/6 cups chicken stock

950 g/2 lbs. 2 oz. purple sprouting or new-season tender broccoli

400 g/14 oz. Mrs Bells Blue or other creamy blue cheese, such as Stilton

a pinch of grated nutmeg

200 ml/¾ cup double/heavy cream

ground black pepper

croutons, to serve

serves 6

Melt the butter in a large saucepan, add the shallots and cook gently for a few minutes to soften. Add the potato and celery, and stir to coat well with the butter. Add the stock and bring the liquid to the boil, then simmer for 15–20 minutes, until the potato is almost tender. Add the broccoli and continue to cook for a further 3–5 minutes, until the stalks are tender. It is crucial not to overcook the broccoli or you lose the lovely bright green colour. Purée the soup immediately with a blender. When smooth, crumble in three quarters of the blue cheese and add a pinch of nutmeg and a good twist of black pepper, to season. (The cheese can be quite salty, so you probably won't need salt, too.) Stir in almost all of the cream, reserving a little to garnish.

Ladle the soup into bowls, garnish with a swirl of cream and crumble over the remaining blue cheese. Serve piping hot as quickly as possible, with croutons.

carrot and fennel soup with fresh lemon, dill and nigella seed

We have been lucky enough to have spent many happy years enjoying our summer holidays in Provence. An old 'mucker' of mine, a crazy Dutchman called Bart, has a family home there. Our respective children remember summers with endless delicious meals under the shade of the 'Abris'. I loved going to the local markets in the morning to buy bread and find inspiration for the day's feast. This is one of the many dishes I created there, with an abundance of ingredients so fresh and filled with Provençal sunshine it makes me feel like returning again and again. Quietly sophisticated with a dramatic fleck of black nigella and olives against the vibrant yellow of the base, the lovely hint of aniseed/anise from the fennel and the tanginess of fresh lemon all work in favour of this wonderful, lively soup.

2 tablespoons extra virgin olive oil, plus extra for drizzling

1 onion, diced

2 garlic cloves, crushed

4 carrots, peeled and diced

½ butternut (or other brightly-fleshed) squash, peeled, deseeded and diced

½ fennel bulb, roughly chopped

800 ml/3⅓ cups vegetable stock

a small bunch of fresh dill, roughly chopped

120 ml/½ cup crème fraîche or plain yogurt

freshly grated zest and freshly squeezed juice of 1 lemon

½ teaspoon nigella seeds (black onion seeds), plus a few extra to garnish

sea salt and ground black pepper

a few very good black olives, finely chopped, to garnish

serves 4–6

Heat the olive oil in a large saucepan and add the onion, garlic, carrots and squash. Toss over high heat until all the vegetables are beginning to soften at the edges. Add the fennel and stock and simmer for about 20 minutes, until the vegetables are tender. Draw the pan off the heat and stir in the fresh dill. Whiz the soup with a stick blender until very smooth. Stir in the crème fraîche and lemon zest and juice, then sprinkle in the nigella seeds. Finally, season to taste.

Serve the soup hot or cold with a scatter of chopped black olives and a few more nigella seeds, and a drizzle of extra virgin olive oil, just to glisten and leave a trail on top of the soup.

Tip: I love to serve this soup with a side dish of chargrilled Provençal vegetable bruschetta. I use the French bread from the day before and bake it for about 7–10 minutes in a cool oven – about 140°C (275°F) Gas 1 – drizzled with olive oil and sprinkled with sea salt. On an open fire (if you have one), barbecue or chargrill, cook fine slices of aubergine/eggplant, peppers, red onion and courgette/zucchini. Layer these on the baked bruschetta and stack with sun blushed tomatoes, black olives and fresh basil. These are a wonderful accompaniment to this delicious sunny soup.

30 g/2 tablespoons butter

1 onion, diced

2 small potatoes, peeled and diced

800 ml/3⅓ cups vegetable stock

300 g/2 generous cups fresh or frozen peas

400 g/14 oz. spinach leaves, any large stalks removed and roughly chopped if large leaves

8–10 fresh mint leaves

2 tablespoons freshly chopped coriander/cilantro

150 ml/⅔ cup double/heavy cream and sour cream combined (for a little more 'edge' use all sour cream, or for a richer soup use all double/heavy cream)

sea salt and ground black pepper

slow-roasted cherry tomatoes, to garnish (optional)

serves 4–6

fresh spinach soup with minted pea and coriander

This is a wow of a soup – as green as the summer fields and as fresh as a handful of herbs! This is one of my original soups, and still 'out-loves' them all. If you want to keep it low in fat, a plain yogurt works just as well as cream, and is perfect if you want to serve this soup chilled for a summer lunch.

Melt the butter in a large saucepan set over gentle heat and add the onion and potatoes. Cook for a few minutes, until the butter has been absorbed and the onion has softened, then pour in the stock and simmer for about 15 minutes, until the potatoes are tender. Add the peas and simmer for a further couple of minutes, until they are just soft, being very careful not to overcook them – it is crucial to keep the peas as green as you can. When the peas are tender, add the fresh spinach and immediately draw the pan off the heat. Blend the soup with a stick blender until almost smooth, then add the fresh herbs and continue to blend until silky smooth. Stir in the double/heavy and sour cream and season to taste with salt and pepper.

Ladle the soup into bowls and scatter with a few slow-cooked oven-dried cherry tomatoes, if using, for a wonderful sweet and dramatic finish.

mother's leek and potato soup

This reminds of being a child – we used to love it when Mum made this delicious, creamy soup. We had a Jersey house cow called Lillian, who was responsible for the lashings of cream, milk and home-churned butter used in our kitchen. You do not need to be so excessive, but restraint is not something my family do well! If you have any leftover ham (hock is best), tear it into bite-size pieces and add to the soup before seasoning and simmer a little while to infuse the flavours. Alternatively, just scatter it on top as a garnish.

50 g/3½ tablespoons butter

4 leeks, whites only, sliced

4 potatoes, peeled and diced

800 m/3⅓ cups chicken or vegetable stock

400 ml/1⅔ cups whole milk

a good slug of double/heavy cream

sea salt and ground black pepper

to garnish

a small handful of fresh parsley, chopped

a small handful of fresh chives, chopped

serves 6–8

Melt the butter in a large saucepan and add the leeks and potatoes. Cook for a few minutes, until the butter has been absorbed and the vegetables have softened. Pour in the stock and milk and simmer for 15–20 minutes, until the potatoes and leeks are tender. Draw the pan off the heat and use a stick blender to blend the soup until it is silky smooth. Stir in the cream and season well with salt and pepper.

To serve, ladle the soup into chunky bowls and garnish with a sprinkling of fresh herbs.

pear, celery and blue cheese soup with salted sugared walnuts and rocket

I would now consider this soup to be rather 'old school', save for the addition of the walnuts and rocket/arugula to bring it up to speed! This is delicious, and great after Christmas to use up that old Stilton, especially accompanied by a shot of sloe gin.

60 g/4 tablespoons salted butter

6 shallots, diced

1 leek, white only, sliced

1 large potato, peeled and diced

½ celeriac/celery root, peeled and diced

1.5 litres/6 cups vegetable stock

6 celery sticks, sliced

2 large pears (hard ones are best for this as less grainy), peeled, cored and roughly diced

400 g/14 oz. blue cheese (Stilton, dolcelatte or similar), crumbled

a small bunch of fresh flat leaf parsley, chopped

2 tablespoons double/heavy cream

ground black pepper

baby rocket/arugula leaves, to serve

for the salted walnuts

½ teaspoon rock salt

1 teaspoon (caster) sugar

a handful of shelled walnuts

a baking sheet, lined with silicone paper

serves 6–8

Melt the butter in a large saucepan and add the shallots, leek, potato and celeriac/celery root. Sauté until just softened and the butter is absorbed, then cover with the stock and add the celery. Simmer for about 15–20 minutes, until all the vegetables are tender, then toss in the pears and most of the blue cheese, reserving a little to garnish. Simmer for a further 3 minutes or so, until the pears are softened, then draw the pan off the heat and blend well with stick blender until smooth. Stir in the chopped parsley, season with black pepper and stir in the cream to enrich the soup.

To make the salted walnut garnish, preheat the oven to 180°C (350°F) Gas 4.

Combine the rock salt and sugar in a pestle and mortar and pound until the salt is ground down to a powder. Put the walnuts in a plastic bag with the salt and sugar powder and shake, shake shake it! Sprinkle the coated nuts onto the prepared baking sheet and toast in the preheated oven for 10–15 minutes until slightly darkened, but do not burn! Leave to cool and as they do they will crisp up.

Serve the soup in rustic bowls, garnished with the salted walnuts, the remaining blue cheese and rocket/arugula leaves.

fennel and courgette soup with parmesan and crème fraîche

This delicious soup was inspired by my love of fennel gratin, a favourite of mine to serve with lamb. I wanted to create the same amazing flavour but in a soup. I added fresh courgettes/zucchini, as we had them growing locally and I wanted to link the soup with produce available close to home. The rocket/arugula gives a lovely peppery hit and the crème fraîche, although rich, lifts the flavour to a slightly fresher note.

75 g/5 tablespoons butter

1 large onion, diced

2 potatoes, peeled and diced

2 small fennel bulbs, finely sliced

2 garlic cloves, crushed

1.75 litres/7⅓ cups vegetable stock

2 courgettes/zucchini, diced

a large handful of rocket/arugula leaves

100 ml/7 tablespoons double/heavy cream

200 ml/¾ cup crème fraîche

2 tablespoons freshly grated Parmesan cheese, plus extra to garnish

sea salt and ground black pepper

a small bunch of fresh parsley, roughly chopped, to garnish

serves 6

Melt the butter in a large saucepan and add the onion, potatoes, fennel and garlic. Cook for a few minutes over medium heat to soften, then pour over the stock. Bring the liquid to a simmer and cook for about 15 minutes, until the fennel is tender. Add the courgettes/zucchini and the rocket/arugula leaves and cook for a further 4 minutes. Draw the pan off the heat and blend with a stick blender until very smooth. Stir in the cream and crème fraîche and the grated Parmesan, and season well with salt and black pepper.

Ladle the soup into bowls and serve garnished with lots of freshly chopped parsley and a sprinkling of Parmesan on top.

beetroot and parsnip soup with horseradish

When I was a child, my great love was playdough. I loved the pots of brightly coloured, sweet-smelling dough; they drew me in, in a multi-sensory way. It was with this memory that I decided to develop my first range of soups in the same vibrant way, to first draw you in with colour in a way so intoxicating that you need to smell, touch and consume... Beetroot/beet was a mainstay in my parent's kitchen garden. My mother would boil and deftly pop the slippery crimson roots from their skins, then slice them thinly and add vinegar before storing in the fridge. So this, my first and still considered my best recipe, does this queen of vegetables proud! And my mum still grows and pickles a mean beetroot.

30 g/2 tablespoons butter

1 small onion, diced

1 small potato, peeled and diced

2 parsnips, peeled and diced

800 ml/3¼ cups vegetable stock

2 large (or 4 small) beetroot/beets, peeled and diced

100 ml/7 tablespoons double/heavy cream and sour cream combined (for a little more 'edge' use all sour cream, or for a richer soup use all double/heavy cream)

1–2 tablespoons horseradish sauce (preferably homemade and the stronger the better)

a pinch of ground ginger, or to taste

sea salt and ground black pepper

serves 6

Melt the butter in a large saucepan set over gentle heat. Add the onion and cook until beginning to soften, then add the potato and parsnips. Pour in the stock and bring to the boil before adding the beetroot/beets. Cover the pan and simmer for about 15 minutes, until all the roots are soft. (Beetroot/beet is very temperature sensitive, so try to make the remainder of the cooking time as quick as possible or the colour will turn brick red rather than the wonderful pink we are aiming for.)

When the vegetables are tender, draw the pan off the heat and blend with a stick blender until a nice nubbly texture is achieved. The parsnips and potato will purée completely, but the beetroot/beet always remains a little grainy – this only adds to the overall texture of the soup, so do not be alarmed!

Stir in the cream and sour cream along with the horseradish and ginger and season with salt and black pepper. Adjust the seasonings to your taste – if you like the heat of ginger or the hit of horseradish, add more! Ladle into bowls and serve.

Tip: For a delicious, punchy garnish, I like to add Japanese wasabi horseradish to some crème fraîche and swirl on top of the soup, then scatter with chives and a few warm cooked edamame beans for a stunning and fun finish.

watercress and asparagus soup with baby broad beans

At the bottom of the field below our house is a wood, and in the wood there is a stream, and in a quiet little off-shoot of the stream there is a watercress bed that has been there since the 'big house' that owned the estate had a team of staff, including cooks and butlers. These watercress beds were a coveted resource and were crucial to the summer menus that the house kitchen produced. This wonderful, ancient bed still produces incredible watercress – strong and peppery and full of iron. I have added other gems from the kitchen garden, in the form of asparagus and baby broad/fava beans. Delicious, elegant and very pretty – and fit for the grandest of tables.

2 bunches of tender asparagus spears

150 g/1¼ cups baby broad/fava beans

100 g/7 tablespoons butter

1½ large onions, chopped

4 potatoes, peeled and diced

1.5 litres/6 cups stock

2 bunches of watercress

a pinch of bicarbonate of soda/baking soda

125 ml/½ cup double/heavy cream, plus extra to serve

sea salt and ground black pepper

serves 6–8

Chop the 'pretty' tip off the asparagus spears and set aside to use as a garnish later. Remove the woody ends from the asparagus by gently bending each stalk – where it naturally breaks is where it becomes tender. Discard the woody ends and chop the tender part of the stems into short lengths.

Remove the broad/fava beans from their tough skins.

Melt the butter in a large saucepan and add the onions and potatoes. Cook until just softening, then cover with the stock. Bring to a simmer and cook for about 15 minutes, until the onions and potatoes are soft. Add the asparagus spears and half of the skinned broad/fava beans and cook until almost tender.

Add the watercress to the pan and almost immediately transfer the soup to a blender (a stick blender doesn't work well, as the watercress clings to the blade, rather annoyingly!) and blend until very smooth. Pour the soup back into the pan, add a pinch of bicarbonate of soda/baking soda (which will help the soup retain its vivid green colour), stir in the cream and season with salt and black pepper.

In a separate saucepan, lightly blanch the reserved asparagus tips and broad/fava beans in boiling water for about 3 minutes – they should still be a vivid green – then drain and pat dry.

To serve, ladle the soup into bowls, swirl through a little cream and garnish with the blanched asparagus tips and beans.

spinach and parmesan soup with nutmeg and rosemary

En Provence in the Luberon, where we spent wonderful summers, there are hedges of rosemary that line the little lanes and tracks, and beg you to find uses for their fragrant, sticky leaves. You can use the tender, washed bags of spinach we find in our supermarkets or a tougher variety such as epinard, with the tough stalks trimmed away. Here, I use a robust cheese in Parmesan, but any other hard, strong cheese would do. The trick, as with so many recipes, is to keep the ingredients in the same company as if they were like-minded people — it makes for a much more harmonious party.

50 g/3½ tablespoons butter

6 strong shallots, chopped

2 garlic cloves, crushed

1 large potato, peeled and diced

2 tablespoons chopped fresh rosemary leaves, plus extra sprigs to garnish

1.5 litres/6 cups chicken stock

1 kg/2¼ lbs. spinach leaves, any really coarse stalks removed and chopped to a manageable size

a pinch of grated nutmeg, plus extra to garnish

200 g/2 cups freshly grated Parmesan cheese, or other hard strong cheese

a few tablespoons of crème fraîche, to taste

sea salt and ground black pepper

serves 6–8

In a large saucepan, melt the butter and gently cook the shallots with the garlic for a few minutes, until softened. Add the potato and rosemary, cover with the stock and bring to a simmer. Cook for 15–20 minutes, until the potato is tender. Add the spinach to the pan and bring to the boil, then draw the pan off the heat and blend everything well with a stick blender. Add a grating of nutmeg, to taste, and season well with salt and pepper. Stir in the Parmesan and most of the crème fraîche, to enrich the soup.

Ladle the soup into bowls and serve garnished with a dusting of nutmeg, a spoonful of the remaining crème fraîche and sprigs of fresh rosemary.

butternut squash soup with orange and ginger

Children's glowing faces, cheeks flushed with excitement, Halloween is the perfect moment to serve this soup. The warming spice and silky smooth texture of the butternut squash is a wonderful golden nectar. Add more spice as you feel the occasion deserves, but perhaps a little less if you are serving to children. Whatever the occasion, this soup is a winner.

55 g/4 tablespoons butter

2 onions, diced

1 large butternut squash (or pumpkin), peeled, deseeded and diced

3 large carrots, peeled and sliced

1 leek, white only, sliced

a good pinch of cumin seeds

a good pinch of garam masala

a good pinch of ground turmeric

a pinch of saffron fronds (optional)

a good pinch of ground ginger or a 1-cm/½-inch piece of fresh ginger, peeled and grated

freshly grated zest and freshly squeezed juice of 1 large orange

1.5 litres/6 cups vegetable stock

350 ml/1⅓ cups sour cream

sea salt and ground black pepper

to garnish

toasted pumpkin seeds

sprigs of fresh thyme or dill

serves 6

Melt the butter in a large saucepan and add the onions, squash, carrots and leek. Toss the vegetables in the butter and cook over medium heat for a few minutes, then stir in the spices and orange zest so that the vegetables are evenly coated. Pour over the stock, cover the pan and simmer for about 15–20 minutes, until the vegetables are tender.

Draw the pan off the heat and blend with a stick blender until very smooth. Stir in the orange juice and sour cream and season to taste with salt and black pepper.

Ladle the soup into bowls and sprinkle with toasted pumpkin seeds and fresh thyme leaves to garnish before serving.

Tip: For a really authentic Halloween look, hollow out a large pumpkin (using the pumkin flesh in the soup in place of the butternut squash), and serve the soup from the pumpkin shell.

parsnip and honey soup with vanilla

A heavenly soup to the eye, and to the palate. Very elegant, interestingly nutty and a little exotic, with vanilla and mace. You must try this one!

50 g/3½ tablespoons butter

2 white onions, chopped

8 parsnips, peeled and diced

2 potatoes, peeled and diced

½ celeriac/celery root, peeled and diced

1.5 litres/6 cups vegetable stock

a pinch of ground ginger

a pinch of ground mace

½ vanilla pod/bean, split

150 ml/⅔ cup double/heavy cream

2 tablespoons honey, or to taste

freshly squeezed juice of ½ lemon, or to taste

serves 6–8

Melt the butter in a large saucepan, add the onions and cook for a few minutes, until softened. Add the parsnips, potatoes and celeriac/celery root to the pan and cover with the stock. Simmer until the vegetables are tender, then stir in the ginger and mace. Remove the pan from the heat and use a stick blender to blend the soup until silky and smooth.

Use a knife to scrape the vanilla seeds from the split pod/bean and add them to the soup. Stir in the cream to enrich the soup, then sweeten to taste with honey and lift the balance with lemon juice. Ladle the soup into bowls and serve – WOW!

chilled cucumber yogurt soup with red chilli and mint salsa

This soup could be considered an aquired taste – but on a warm summer's day it is easy to aquire! It is deliciously refreshing, with a kick from the chilli salsa.

1 tablespoon butter

4 shallots, diced

2 cucumbers, peeled and deseeded

a small bunch of fresh dill, chopped

leaves from a few sprigs of fresh mint, chopped

a small bunch of fresh chives, chopped

1 slice of white bread

3 tomatoes, peeled, deseeded and diced

400 g/1¾ cups thick Greek yogurt

200 ml/¾ cup double/heavy cream

1 litre/4 cups vegetable stock

½ teaspoon cumin seeds

½ teaspoon caraway seeds

grated zest of 1 lemon

2 teaspoons Dijon mustard

sea salt and ground black pepper

for the salsa

2 red chillies, finely diced

a squeeze of lemon juice

a drizzle of olive oil

serves 6–8

In a small frying pan, melt the butter and sauté the shallots for a few minutes, until softened, then leave to cool.

Cut a small chunk from one of the cucumbers and set aside to use in the salsa, along with a little of each of the chopped herbs.

Put the shallots and all the other soup ingredients in a blender and whiz until smooth – the soup should be the consistency of double/heavy cream. The herbs need to be a balance of all three – although the mint will be fairly dominant in the overall freshness and flavour of the soup – so taste and add more of any herb that may be lacking. Season to taste with salt and black pepper, then put the soup in the fridge to chill for at least 1 hour before serving.

To make the salsa, finely dice the reserved cucumber. Combine it with the red chilli and reserved herbs. Mix with a little lemon juice and a drizzle of olive oil to bind, then chill until needed.

Serve the soup in small chilled glasses with a teaspoon and garnish with the pretty chilli and herb salsa.

lettuce and courgette soup with chervil

The understated nature of this soup makes it special. I used to make this in the summer when Terry and I ran the little gastropub, The Foresters Arms, in the beautiful Coverdale. It is inspired by Raymond Blanc, who was my hero. It mixes simplicity with opulence... much like the customers we attracted in the pub – from elegant diners to red-faced farmers! This soup can be eaten hot or cold, so you can adapt it to the unpredictable weather.

12 sweet shallots, diced

1 large potato, peeled and diced

40 g/3 tablespoons butter

1.5 litres/6 cups chicken or vegetable stock

2 garlic cloves, crushed

4 courgettes/zucchini, diced

1 large, plump flat lettuce or large Little Gem/Bibb lettuces, finely sliced

200 ml/¾ cup double/heavy cream

a good bunch of fresh chervil, chopped, plus a few whole leaves to garnish

a squeeze of lemon juice

sea salt and ground black pepper

serves 6–8

In a large heavy based saucepan, sweat the shallots and potato in the butter for a few minutes, until they are softened. Pour in the stock and add the garlic, then simmer for about 15 minutes, until the potato is tender. Add the courgettes/zucchini to the pan and continue to simmer for a further 2–3 minutes, until the they are just tender but still nice and bright green. Do not overcook, as the colour will fade and the freshness of flavour will be lost.

Add the lettuce to the pan, then draw the pan off the heat. Using a stick blender, purée the soup until nice and smooth. Stir in the cream and chopped chervil, season to taste with salt and black pepper and sharpen the soup with a squeeze of lemon juice.

Ladle the soup into bowls and serve garnished with a few chervil leaves.

tomato and red pepper soup with wensleydale cheese

I live in Wensleydale in the English countryside and the Hawes creamery has been a part of our life for as long as we can remember. The texture of Wensleydale cheese is unique, and is really the very best for this soup – its lovely creamy but tangy flavour and springy texture contrasts perfectly with the sweet tomato and red pepper base. If you can't find Wensleydale, a not-too-salty feta would be the next best choice. This soup is wonderfully versatile and can be used as a base for a pasta sauce or chilli, too. Make it your own, or enjoy it as it is!

2 tablespoons olive oil, plus extra for drizzling

1 small onion, diced

1 garlic clove, crushed

1 red pepper, deseeded and diced

700 g/1 lb. 9 oz. fresh tomatoes, finely chopped, or canned chopped tomatoes

800 ml/3⅓ cups vegetable stock

a pinch of paprika

a few sprigs of fresh basil, plus a few extra leaves to garnish

90 g/6 tablespoons tomato purée/paste

sea salt and ground black pepper

reduced balsamic vinegar, for drizzling

250 g/9 oz. Wensleydale cheese, diced, to serve

serves 6

Heat the olive oil in a large saucepan, throw in the onion, garlic and red pepper and cook for a few minutes, until softened. Add all but 120 g/4 oz. of the tomatoes and pour over the stock. Stir in a pinch of paprika – not too much, as this is just to give a little warmth, not any great heat! – and add the basil. Cover and simmer for about 15 minutes.

Draw the pan off the heat and blend with a stick blender until smooth, then add the reserved chopped tomato and the tomato purée/paste. Cook for a few more minutes to warm the tomatoes through, then season with salt and black pepper.

Ladle the soup into warmed soup bowls and scatter cubes of Wensleydale cheese over the soup, along with a few leaves of fresh basil. Drizzle with a little olive oil and a few drops of reduced balsamic vinegar for a dramatic finish.

field mushroom soup with parmesan, thyme and pancetta

I inherited my gluttony from my father, who LOVES his food! He cooked a lot when we were small, usually something very rich, full of butter and cream. When field mushrooms were popping up, he was in heaven – and thrilled with his excuse to get behind the frying pan! Laden with flat black-bottomed mushrooms as big as a small plate, he would throw in butter, then cream, then reduce it down and add splashes of Worcestershire sauce. After this, he popped everything in the oven, covered in cheese and with a scattering of fresh herbs. I have added crisp pancetta to this idea, based on Daddy's over-the-top deliciousness, but the thought behind this is for him!

100 g/7 tablespoons butter

1 onion, diced

1 garlic clove, crushed

6 small waxy potatoes, peeled and diced

8 large flat field mushrooms, sliced

800 ml/3⅓ cups vegetable stock

a muslin/cheesecloth bag filled with bay leaves, a few juniper berries, sprigs of fresh thyme and a few black peppercorns, tied with string

150 ml/⅝ cup double/heavy cream, plus a little extra to serve

a dollop of Dijon mustard, to taste

150 g/5½ oz. dry-cured bacon, cooked until crispy and cut into long pieces

50 g/½ cup freshly grated Parmesan cheese

fresh thyme leaves, to garnish

Melt the butter in a large saucepan, add the onion, garlic and potatoes and cook until the onion is softened, but do not allow to brown. Add the field mushrooms and toss around until they start to wilt. (Mushrooms are very greedy with butter and tend to suck it all up while they are deciding to cook, then spit it all out again when they have relented to soften. If you have yourself some particularly greedy mushrooms, you may need to add a little more butter.) When the mushrooms have eventually settled down and reduced in size, pour over the stock. Add your little muslin/cheescloth bag of infusion, cover the pan and turn the heat down to a very low simmer. Somehow the longer this cooks the better it is; mushrooms are fussy creatures and do not like being rushed!

When the flavours have married – this should take about 40 minutes – draw the pan off the heat and remove the muslin/cheesecloth bag. Stir in the cream and mustard, then blend with a stick blender until smooth.

Serve the soup in big rustic bowls and add a swirl of cream to contrast against the dark grey of the mushrooms. Garnish with the bacon pieces, a sprinkling of Parmesan and a few fresh thyme leaves. Extra bacon and cheese would, of course, also be quite acceptable!

serves 6

annabel's pheasant soup

Annabel is an amazing person; artistic, creative and kind, she taught all my boys to write beautifully, and my youngest son to read and write, get through his English exams, and how to appreciate both brains and beauty! She claims not to be able to cook, but years ago she asked me to help her with a dinner party where she had prepared the pheasant dish that was the inspiration for this deliciously rich soup. It is, to this day, the nicest pheasant recipe I have ever had, and deserves pole position in this book – as does she!

for the marinade

500 ml/2 cups ruby Port

2 red onions, finely chopped

2 garlic cloves, crushed

2 bay leaves

a few sprigs of fresh thyme

6 juniper berries, slightly crushed to release their flavour

for the soup

1 large pheasant, skinned and jointed

50–75 g/3½–5 tablespoons butter

1.5 litres/6 cups game stock (follow the recipe for Beef Stock on page 11, using duck, pigeon, pheasant, partridge and venison bones, or a mixture)

500 g/1 lb. 2 oz. chestnut, shiitake or button mushrooms, or a mixture

1 tablespoon cornflour/cornstarch

2 egg yolks

250 ml/1 cup double/heavy cream

sea salt and ground black pepper

croutons, to serve

a large flameproof casserole dish

serves 6–8

Combine all the marinade ingredients in a dish and add the pheasant joints. Make sure all the meat is covered in the marinade and leave for 8 hours or overnight in the fridge.

When ready to make the soup, remove the pheasant joints from the marinade and dry thoroughly with paper towels. Reserve the marinade.

Heat 1–2 tablespoons of the butter in the casserole dish and cook the joints until nicely browned. Pour over the reserved marinade, along with the game stock. Set the dish over low heat and poach the pheasant very gently for 1½ hours.

Remove the pheasant joints from the liquid (reserving the liquid) and allow to cool. Shred all the meat from the bones, being careful that all the bones are removed. Set the meat aside.

Heat the remaining butter in a frying pan and sauté the mushrooms gently, giving a little colour, then set aside.

Strain the poaching liquid, discarding the bits, and pour it into a clean pan. Bring the liquid to a very gentle simmer, then add the shredded meat and mushrooms.

In a small bowl, combine the cornflour/cornstarch, egg yolks and cream and mix to a smooth paste. Stir the mixture into the simmering liquid and allow to just thicken, then draw the pan off the heat. Season with salt and black pepper.

Ladle the soup into bowls and serve with old-fashioned croutons on the side.

game consommé with softly boiled quails' eggs and brioche

When I was a lass, cutting my teeth on the London scene, I had a client who asked me to make this game consommé for dinner. I was terrified, as consommé conjures up the same fear in me as a soufflé does to the non-cook. However, it seemed to go down rather well, and the addition of quails' eggs and brioche makes the effort worthwhile. If you want to really push the boat out, serve with pâté de foie gras to spread on the brioche.

4 egg whites

400 g/14 oz. minced/ground chicken

2 onions, diced

1 leek, sliced

2 celery sticks, sliced

1 garlic clove, chopped

4 litres/quarts game stock (follow the recipe for Beef Stock on page 11, using duck, pigeon, pheasant, partridge and venison bones, or a mixture)

12 juniper berries, slightly crushed to release their flavour

a good sprig of fresh thyme

2 bay leaves

2 tablespoons tomato purée/paste

a splash of dry sherry, to taste

sea salt and ground black pepper

to serve

8 slices of brioche, buttered on both sides and sliced into fingers

8 quails' or gulls' eggs

a small pot of pâté de foie gras (optional)

a deep, narrow stock pan

a muslin/cheesecloth-lined sieve/ strainer or jelly bag

serves 8

Put the egg whites in a mixing bowl and gently whisk to loosen them and create bubbles.

Put the chicken, all the vegetables and the garlic in the bowl of a food processor and pulse until a rough paste is achieved. Pour in the egg white and blitz for a further 3 seconds only. Transfer to a bowl, cover and chill for 10 minutes.

Pour the stock into the stock pan and add the juniper berries, thyme, bay leaves and tomato purée/paste. Bring the liquid to a boil, then reduce to a simmer. Add the chicken mixture and incorporate it into the stock with a balloon whisk, making sure it is well dispersed throughout the stock. Bring the liquid to a boil and keep it at a steady rolling boil until the liquid has reduced to half the volume. During cooking, a white crust with a dirty, silty look to it will form on top of the liquid. Small holes will appear in the crust, being forced open by the heat and steam of the stock beneath. Towards the end of the simmering time, very carefully prise open one of the holes in the crust to check that the liquid beneath is clear. When satisfied that the clarity has been achieved, carefully lift the crust off the liquid with a large slotted spoon. Strain the consommé through the muslin/ cheesecloth-lined sieve/strainer into a clean pan.

When ready to serve the consommé, heat it through very gently (don't let it boil or it will go cloudy), add a good splash of dry sherry and season with salt and black pepper.

Preheat the oven to 190°C (375°F) Gas 5. Lay the buttered brioche slices on a baking sheet and bake in the oven for 5–7 minutes, until crisp and golden.

To boil the quails' eggs, pop them in a pan of cold water and set over medium heat. When the water reaches simmering point, draw the pan off the heat and leave the eggs to sit in the hot water for 1 minute. Drain off the water and gently peel the eggs.

Ladle the soup into tureens and pop a boiled quails' egg into each one. Serve with the hot toasted buttered brioche and pâté de foie gras, if wished. Excellent!

pumpkin soup with cep mushrooms

This is a deliciously rich and smooth soup with a colour of deep vibrant gold. I had a similar dish at a Gordon Ramsay restaurant as an amuse bouche, and that is where the idea came from. This is less rich, but every bit as delicious and surprising. The silky nature of the cep works so well with the smooth soup. Truffle oil finishes this off and elevates it from the everyday to something really special - but this is at your discretion.

50 g/3½ tablespoons butter

2 white onions, diced

2 garlic cloves, finely chopped

1 small pumpkin, peeled, deseeded and diced

½ butternut squash, peeled, deseeded and diced

1.5 litres/6 cups vegetable stock

2 cep mushrooms, finely sliced

200 ml/¾ cup double/heavy cream

sea salt and ground black pepper

for the garnish

truffle oil, for drizzling (optional)

chopped fresh parsley

fresh thyme leaves

serves 6

Melt about three-quarters of the butter in a large saucepan and cook the onions, garlic, pumpkin and squash until soft. Add the stock to the pan and bring to a boil. Reduce the heat and simmer for about 15 minutes, until the pumpkin and squash are cooked. Take the pan off the heat and blitz the mixture to a purée with a stick blender.

In a frying pan, heat the remaining butter and fry the ceps very gently for a few minutes, until softened but without colouring. Add the ceps to the soup and stir in the cream, then season to taste with salt and black pepper. Ladle the soup into bowls and serve garnished with a sprinkle of fresh parsley and thyme leaves and a little drizzle of truffle oil, if you wish.

guinea fowl risotto with porcini mushrooms, pumpkin and thyme

I think guinea fowl is one of the very best eating birds to be had. It is massively superior in flavour to chicken, and less polarizing than other stronger game birds. Here, in this satisfying, soupy risotto, it is succulent full flavoured and delicious.

100 g/3½ oz. dried porcini mushrooms

1 guinea fowl

1 onion, diced

1 carrot, peeled and diced

2 celery sticks, diced

a bunch of fresh thyme, plus leaves from another small bunch

4 garlic cloves, 1 bashed and 3 crushed

½ small pumpkin, peeled, deseeded and diced

100 ml/7 tablespoons olive oil

2 red onions, diced

250 g/1¼ cups Arborio risotto rice

600 g/1 lb. 5 oz. mixed fresh mushrooms, including shiitake, sliced

15 g/1 tablespoon butter

100 ml/7 tablespoons white wine

a small bunch of fresh parsley, chopped

a squeeze of lemon juice, to taste

200 g/2 cups freshly grated Parmesan cheese

sea salt and ground black pepper

serves 6–8

Soak the dried porcini mushrooms in a little water for at least 1 hour. Once rehydrated, drain (reserve the soaking water) and chop down any very large mushrooms.

Put the guinea fowl in a large saucepan and add the onion, carrot, celery, bunch of thyme and the bashed garlic clove. Pour over 2 litres/quarts water, set the pan over medium heat and bring to a simmer. Poach the guinea fowl very gently for about 1½ hours, until it is cooked and very tender, and the meat is falling off the bone. Remove the bird from the pan and strain the liquid, reserving the stock to use later. Once the guinea fowl is cool, strip all the flesh from the carcass and set aside.

Preheat the oven to 190°C (375°F) Gas 5.

Put the diced pumpkin in a large roasting pan and drizzle with a little of the olive oil. Roast in the preheated oven for 15–20 minutes, until tender and golden.

Heat the remaining oil in large heavy-based saucepan, add the red onions and crushed garlic and cook for a few minutes, until softened. Add the rice, stir to coat in the oil and cook for a further minute, then add the rehydrated porcini, sliced fresh mushrooms and the butter. Cook until the mushrooms have wilted, then pour in the reserved guinea fowl stock and porcini soaking water. Simmer, stirring often, for about 12–15 minutes, until the rice is almost cooked, adding more water if needed – the soup should be thick, but loose enough to spoon into a bowl. When the rice is almost tender, add the shredded guinea fowl meat, roast pumpkin and white wine and cook for a further couple of minutes, until the rice is perfectly cooked and the meat and pumpkin are warmed through.

Season with salt and pepper and add the parsley and thyme leaves, then lift the flavour with a squeeze of lemon juice. Lastly, stir in half of the Parmesan and serve the soup with remainder on the side, for sprinkling.

chilled smoked salmon, avocado and chive soup

This is a lovely way to enjoy avocado in the summer and a real treat for lunch with hot crusty garlic bread. Avocado, salmon and chives are a marriage made in heaven and really worth a try.

Trim the greens from the spring onions/scallions and set them aside to use in the salsa. Roughly chop the spring onion/scallion whites and put them in the bowl of a food processor along with the avocado, garlic, green chillies, cucumber, cream cheese, sour cream and about one-quarter of the stock to loosen. Blitz on full speed until smooth, then pour into a large bowl and stir in the remaining stock slowly, to achieve a good even consistency – it should not be too thin, but should coat the back of a spoon. Avocados vary and the soup's consistency will depend on their fatty or more watery nature, so you may not need to add all of the stock.

Season the soup with salt and pepper and add the smoked salmon (reserve a few ribbons to garnish), the finely snipped chives and a good squeeze of fresh lime juice to balance the acidity and richness. Cover the soup and chill.

To make the salsa garnish, finely chop the reserved spring onion/scallion greens, put them in a mixing bowl with all the salsa ingredients and mix gently.

Serve a generous amount of avocado soup with a lovely spoonful of salsa piled in the centre and a few of the reserved salmon ribbons to garnish.

5 spring onions/scallions

5 ripe avocados, peeled, stoned/pitted and diced

2 garlic cloves, crushed

2 green chillies, sliced

½ cucumber, peeled, deseeded and diced

60 g/¼ cup cream cheese

60 g/¼ cup sour cream

1 litre/4 cups vegetable or chicken stock

5 slices of smoked salmon, cut into fine ribbons and any brown meat removed

a small bunch of fresh chives, finely snipped

a squeeze of lime juice, to taste

sea salt and ground black pepper

for the salsa garnish

a small bunch of fresh coriander/cilantro, chopped

grated zest and freshly squeezed juice of 1 lime

2 tablespoons olive oil

4 ripe tomatoes, peeled (see tip, page 117), deseeded and finely diced

½ red onion, finely diced

¼ cucumber, finely diced

serves 6–8

celery, pine nut and smoked chicken soup with lemon & rocket

Tom Dick (real name I promise!), whose mother kindly spared him the addition of Harry, has been my head chef and number one man for some 15 years. A Scott to his boots, Tom can turn his hand to anything you ask him to make. He cut his young culinary teeth in the Army, then in private game and fishing lodges, before losing a fair few of them on the rugby pitch! This little marvel of a soup demonstrates Tom's ability to take something special and make it even more so. He rustled it up for us one day for an impromptu gourmet lunch – it was a surprise, and a very good one! It contains all the things I love best in a sandwich, except the bread! A fantastic summer lunch soup or appetizer – delicious!

50 g/3½ tablespoons butter

1 head of celery, chopped

4 onions, diced

5 potatoes, peeled and diced

2 litres/quarts chicken stock

a large handful of rocket/arugula leaves, plus extra to garnish

a small bunch of fresh thyme, leaves only

2 smoked chicken breasts, diced

3 tablespoons toasted pine nuts, plus extra to garnish

250 g/1 cup crème fraîche

2 tablespoons creamed horseradish

grated zest and freshly squeezed juice of 1 lemon

a large bunch of fresh parsley, chopped

a handful of fresh chives, snipped

sea salt and ground black pepper

shaved Parmesan cheese, to garnish

serves 6

Melt the butter in a large saucepan, add the celery, onions and potatoes and cook over gentle heat for a few minutes, until softened. Pour over the stock, cover the pan and simmer for about 15–20 minutes, until the potatoes and celery are tender.

Draw the pan off the heat and blend the soup with a stick blender until smooth. Add the rocket/arugula and continue to blend until it is well dispersed (a little texture left in is nice). Sprinkle over the fresh thyme leaves and stir in the diced chicken, pine nuts, crème fraîche and creamed horseradish. Lift the flavour with lemon zest and juice and season with a little salt and a good amount of black pepper. Finally, stir in the chopped parsley and snipped chives.

Ladle the soup into bowls and serve garnished with a few more toasted pine nuts, a few leaves of rocket/arugula and Parmesan shavings.

cream of celeriac and white bean soup with toasted hazelnuts and truffle oil

I love soups that are visually honest, then when you taste them it's almost like a game of 'what is that flavour coming through?' This is one of those soups. I adore the ugly brute that is celeriac; it has such a wonderful nutty sweetness. The starch from the smooth white beans gives the soup richness, while the hazelnuts and truffle oil work to bring both texture and forest-floor flavours.

150 g/1 cup hazelnuts

90 ml/6 tablespoons olive oil

8 banana shallots, finely diced

2 garlic cloves, roughly chopped

2 celeriac/celery root, peeled and diced

2 celery sticks, sliced

2 bay leaves

2 litres/quarts chicken stock

a 400-g/14-oz. can cannellini beans, drained

180 ml/¾ cup double/heavy cream

a squeeze of lemon juice, to taste

sea salt and ground black pepper

truffle oil, for drizzling

serves 6–8

To toast the hazelnuts, put them in a roasting pan and pop them in a medium–hot oven for about 10 minutes, until they are just golden and smelling lovely. Tip the toasted nuts into a tea/dish towel and rub well to remove the skins, then roughly chop them.

Put the olive oil, shallots, garlic, celeriac/celery root, celery and bay leaves in a saucepan and toss over medium–high heat for a few minutes, until beginning to soften. Add the stock to the pan along with three-quarters of the toasted hazelnuts and the cannellini beans. Cover the pan and simmer gently for about 15–20 minutes, until the celeriac/celery root is very tender. Draw the pan off the heat and remove the bay leaves.

With a stick blender, whiz the soup until very smooth, then stir in the cream and blend briefly again until well mixed. If you think the soup is a little thin, allow to simmer gently over very low heat to reduce down a little – this should be a smooth, velvety soup. When you are happy with the consistency, season with salt and pepper and lift the flavour with a squeeze of lemon juice.

Ladle the soup into bowls, scatter the reserved chopped hazelnuts over the top and drizzle with truffle oil to serve.

cream of potato and roasted red onion soup with salted caramel

This soup is a little unusual, and quite a surprise! Salted caramel has a real wow factor and is delicious with both sweet and savoury food. The roasted red onions add visual drama against the quiet of the potato base. You don't have to finish with a swirl; you could serve the caramel on the side for people to add as much as they like, but a swirl makes more of a talking point!

65 g/4½ tablespoons butter

1 small white onion, diced

5 large potatoes, peeled and diced

3 parsnips, peeled and diced

1 litre/4 cups chicken or vegetable stock

500 ml/2 cups double/heavy cream

2 large red onions, diced

leaves from a few sprigs of fresh thyme

sea salt and ground black pepper

for the salted caramel

200 g/1 cup caster/granulated sugar

40 g/3 tablespoons salted butter

250 ml/1 cup double/heavy cream

serves 6

Melt 50 g/3½ tablespoons of the butter in a large saucepan, add the white onion, potatoes and parsnips and cook over gentle heat for a few minutes, until softened. Pour over the stock, cover the pan and simmer for about 15–20 minutes, until the potatoes and parsnips are tender. Strain the vegetables (reserving the liquid), and transfer them to a blender. Blitz them with the cream until puréed and smooth, then gradually pour in the reserved cooking stock, blending continuously until a rich smooth base is achieved – it should be quite thick and leave a trail when a spoon is passed through it.

Preheat the oven to 200°C (400°F) Gas 6.

Put the red onions and thyme leaves on a baking sheet with the remaining butter and roast in the preheated oven for about 10–15 minutes, until soft and tender, turning once. Set aside.

To make the salted caramel, put the sugar in a heavy-based saucepan and set over medium–high heat. Leave to heat for about 5–7 minutes, until the sugar has dissolved and turned from white to pale golden (you may need to tilt the pan slightly and very gently swirl the sugar a little to allow an even colour to be achieved). As soon as the caramel is pale golden, draw the pan off the heat and stir in the butter and cream. Turn the heat down to medium, and return the pan to the heat for 3–5 minutes to allow the colour to enrich to a golden caramel, gently swirling it around the pan to prevent it from burning. Add a pinch of sea salt and, while still warm, pour into a small plastic jug/pitcher.

To assemble, heat the soup base and add the roasted red onions, then stir in a little of the salted caramel to sweeten, to taste. Ladle the soup into serving bowls or mugs and, with a spoon, make a swirl of salted caramel on top. Any remaining caramel can be served on the side or saved and used again – just keep it covered in the fridge for up to a few weeks.

jerusalem artichoke soup with sorrel and sage

My rather mad journalist friend Jonny Beardsall makes all number of things from artichokes as he has them growing like weeds in his garden. Commonly known as 'fartichokes' for very obvious reasons, they have a unique flavour, and the acidity of the sorrel is a sublime combination. This is one of Jonny's staples. When having eaten, stand well back and choose who you spend the evening with very carefully!

150 g/1¼ sticks butter

about 16 Jerusalem artichokes, peeled and sliced

1 carrot, peeled and sliced

1 small leek, white only, sliced

2 celery sticks, sliced

4 shallots, sliced

2 litres/quarts vegetable stock

leaves from a sprig of fresh sage

300 ml/1¼ cups double/heavy cream

8 large sorrel leaves, finely shredded

sea salt and ground black pepper

for the garnish

vegetable oil, for deep-frying

6 Jerusalem artichokes, peeled and cut into 'chips'

20 fresh sage leaves

serves 6

Melt the butter in a large saucepan and add all the vegetables. Toss them around to coat in the butter and cook for a few minutes, until softening at the edges. Pour over the stock and add the sage leaves. Cover the pan and simmer for 15–20 minutes, until all the vegetables are tender. Draw the pan off the heat and blend with a stick blender until smooth. Stir in the cream and season with salt and black pepper.

To make the garnish, heat enough oil for deep-frying until very hot in a large saucepan and deep-fry the artichoke chips for 3–5 minutes, until golden and crisp. Fish them out with a slotted spoon and drain on paper towels. Add the sage leaves to the oil and fry for 2–3 seconds only, until crisp, then fish them out and drain those, too. Sprinkle the artichoke chips and sage leaves with plenty of sea salt and keep warm to serve on top of the soup.

Just before serving, stir the sorrel into the soup (it will discolour if you do this any sooner).

Ladle the soup into bowls and serve garnished with the crispy artichoke chips and sage leaves.

citrus broth with chilli, ginger and king prawn

This is such a fresh and healthy broth, it almost does you good just to read the recipe! It will give you a glow in your cheeks and leave you feeling energized and ready to go. You can try it with any other shellfish, too, or scallops or firm white fish would also be delicious. If you cannot find straw mushrooms, use shiitake or another variety of Chinese mushroom – the weirder they look, the better the soup will look!

for the broth

2 litres/quarts chicken or fish stock

6 lemongrass stalks, bashed to release their flavour

2 red chillies, split (seeds and all)

6 fresh kaffir lime leaves

1 tablespoon sliced fresh ginger

8 spring onions/scallions, sliced

for the soup

2–3 tablespoons ground nut oil

500 g/1 lb. 2 oz. raw green king prawns/jumbo shrimp, shelled

3 garlic cloves, finely sliced

1 tablespoon very finely sliced fresh ginger

1 green chilli, finely diced

1 red chilli, finely diced

250 g/9 oz. straw or mixed exotic Chinese mushrooms, finely sliced

2 fresh kaffir lime leaves

10 spring onions/scallions, whites and greens separated, sliced

4–5 tablespoons fish sauce

1–2 tablespoons soy sauce

freshly squeezed juice of 1 lime

a small bunch of fresh coriander/cilantro, leaves only

200 g/7 oz. mange tout/snow peas or sugar snap peas, sliced on the angle

sea salt and ground black pepper

lime wedges, to serve

serves 6

To make the broth, put all the broth ingredients in a large saucepan and bring the liquid to a simmer. Continue to simmer for 15 minutes or so with the pan covered until an aromatic infusion has been achieved, then pass the broth through a sieve/strainer to remove the seasonings. Set the broth aside until required.

Heat the oil in a large saucepan and add the prawns/shrimp along with the garlic, ginger, green and red chillies and mushrooms. Toss around until all are well coated in the oil and cook for about 3–5 minutes, until the prawns/shrimp are beginning to turn pink. Pour over the broth, then add the lime leaves, spring onion/scallion whites, fish sauce and soy sauce, and simmer for a further 3–5 minutes.

Add most of the lime juice, taste and then add more lime juice or soy sauce if you feel the seasoning is not sufficient. When happy with the flavour – the soup should be hot, salty and sour – stir in the coriander/cilantro, spring onion/scallion greens and sugar snap peas.

Ladle generous servings of the broth into bowls and serve with lime wedges on the side.

callaloo with sorrel and crab

When I worked in the Caribbean, I fell in love with every aspect of the cuisine, except the popular callaloo soup, which is generally made with a bitter green leaf similar to spinach. I set out to make my own version that was sweeter and more interesting but which still captured the character of the Caribbean. The sorrel gives the same bitter note as the callaloo, but the spinach is kinder, and the crab is clean and fresh and gives a lovely sweetness against the bitter notes of the leaves. If you don't like or can't find okra, you can use courgette/zucchini instead and cut down the simmering time to about 7–10 minutes.

250 g/9 oz. white crab meat

grated zest and freshly squeezed juice of 1½ limes

150 g/5½ oz. fresh sorrel leaves, finely sliced

25 g/2 tablespoons salted butter

1 onion, finely sliced

3 garlic cloves, crushed

175 g/6 oz. okra, sliced

2 red chillies, finely sliced into strips

1.25 litres/5 cups fish stock

250 g/9 oz. brown crab meat

a 400-g/14-oz. can coconut milk or a 250-g/9-oz. pack coconut cream

a dash of soy sauce, to taste

a dash of fish sauce, to taste

1 green chilli, finely sliced, or a pinch of chilli powder (optional)

250 g/9 oz. baby spinach leaves

5 spring onions/scallions, finely sliced into strips

½ sweet red pepper, finely sliced

a dash of double/heavy cream (optional)

sea salt and ground black pepper

grated nutmeg, to garnish

serves 6

Put the white crab meat, lime zest and sorrel in a small bowl with a squeeze of the lime juice to 'loosen' the mixture, and leave in the fridge until needed.

Melt the butter in a large saucepan and add the onion, garlic and okra. Sauté for a few minutes, until just soft, then add the red chillies, stock and brown crab meat. Simmer very gently for 15–20 minutes, until the okra is tender. (The okra will very slightly thicken the soup.) Add the coconut milk or cream and stir until all lumps are incorporated.

I feel that this is the best stage to season the soup, and even though there are other fairly punchy ingredients still to come, it is at its most robust at this point. Add a splash each of soy sauce and fish sauce and the remaining lime juice. If you would like a little more heat, add the fresh green chilli (to give better flavour and more subtle heat) or a pinch of chilli powder. When you are happy with the balance of heat, salt (from the soy) and acid (from the lime), add the fresh spinach. When the spinach is wilted, add the spring onions/scallions and red pepper and cook for a couple of minutes. Finally, stir in the white crab meat mixture and the cream, if using.

Spoon the callaloo into generous bowls and serve with a dusting of grated nutmeg on top for a truly Caribbean finish!

lobster bisque à la belinda

2 large cooked lobsters (if home-cooked, keep the boiling water for stock)

150 g/1¼ sticks butter

2 onions, diced

4 small potatoes, peeled and diced

1 fennel bulb, sliced

4 celery sticks, sliced

1 large leek, white only, sliced

4 garlic cloves, crushed

a 2.5-cm/1-inch piece of fresh ginger, peeled and grated, or a good pinch of ground ginger (optional)

2 bay leaves

2 sprigs of fresh tarragon or 1 generous teaspoon dried

2 litres/quarts fish stock (made with the lobster poaching water, if home-cooked – see page 8)

200 g/7 oz. fresh or canned chopped tomatoes

200 ml/¾ cup white wine

4 tablespoons tomato purée/paste

150 ml/⅔ cup vermouth plus 150 ml/⅔ cup Cognac, or 300 ml/1¼ cups of either

a good pinch of cayenne pepper

a dash of Tabasco (optional)

250 g/1 cup double/heavy cream, plus a little extra to garnish

a squeeze of lemon juice, to taste

sea salt and ground black pepper

freshly snipped chives, to garnish

serves 6

This bisque is the epitome of decadence – lobster with cream and brandy. It's not an everyday dish, but definitely one to prepare once in a while, for very special occasions. So, every cook should have a recipe for when that moment comes – and here it is... If you like, you can cheat and replace one of the lobsters with some white and dark crab meat, adding the meat just before serving.

Remove all the meat from the cooked lobster tails and claws, and set aside. Reserve the shells to flavour the soup.

Melt the butter in a large saucepan and add all the vegetables, garlic, ginger and herbs, then add the lobster shells. Pour in the stock, tomatoes and white wine, cover the pan and leave to simmer gently with the lid on for about 1 hour.

Now, some people liquidize the shell and all, but if you, like me, worry about the sharpness of the blade on your stick blender, remove the shells from the pan, and blend all the other bits until smooth. If brave, and have strong blades, you can whiz the lot! Pass the soup through a fine-meshed sieve/strainer twice, using a ladle to force the purée through to achieve a fine smooth base. Pour the soup into a clean pan and stir in the tomato purée/paste.

Put the vermouth and Cognac in a separate small pan and set over high heat. Very carefully flambé the liquid by using a long kitchen match to set the alcohol alight. Simply touch a lit match to the very edge of the pan and the alcohol fumes will catch – stand well back! The flames will die down once all the alcohol has burned away. When this has happened, pour the remaining liquid into the soup.

Add the cayenne pepper and a little splash of Tabasco, if you like it hot. Stir in the cream and a squeeze of lemon juice to lift the flavour, then season with salt and black pepper. Lastly, and just before you want to eat it, gently warm the soup to a simmer and add the reserved lobster meat to heat through.

Serve the soup in elegant bowls, garnished with a swirl of cream and snipped chives.

Tip: If your lobster bisque is a tiny bit bitter, add a little sugar to bring back the balance.

watercress soup with nashi pear, scallops and pancetta

The inspiration for this soup came from my days in Western Australia, while working in the restaurant at the Leeuwin Estate Vineyard. Leeuwin were famous for their fantastic wines, and for the equally fantastic concert in the magnificent grounds. A celebrity chef would develop a special menu for the occasion, and the year I was there it was the turn of Stephanie Alexander, of Melbourne restaurant fame. She did a dish with Nashi pears and scallops, and it is with that in mind that I created this soup. The texture of the pears is unique, very crunchy, which contrasts beautifully with the soft richness of the scallops.

50 g/3½ tablespoons butter

6 shallots, finely sliced

2 standard pears, peeled, cored and diced

1.75 litres/7⅓ cups vegetable stock

2 big bunches of watercress, well chopped

400 ml/1⅔ cups double/heavy cream

sea salt and ground black pepper

for the garnish

8 slices of pancetta

8 king scallops

1 tablespoon butter

2 Nashi pears

a baking sheet, lined with baking paper

serves 6

Melt the butter in a large saucepan and add the shallots and pears. Sauté for 4–5 minutes to soften, but do not allow to colour. Pour in the stock, bring to a simmer and cook for about 8 minutes, until the shallots and pears are tender. Add the watercress and use a spatula to push it down until it is submerged in the liquid and wilted a little (cook for no more than 2 minutes longer so that it retains its vivid green), then draw the pan off the heat. Whiz the soup with a stick blender until very smooth, then pour into a clean pan, stir in the cream and season with salt and pepper.

For the garnish, preheat the oven to 190°C (375°F) Gas 5. Lay the slices of pancetta on the prepared baking sheet and bake in the preheated oven for about 10 minutes, until crisp, being careful not to let them burn. Set aside until needed.

Prepare the scallops by removing any membrane and wiping with paper towels. Leave the corals on, if you wish, or remove them for a cleaner look. Slice the scallops in half horizontally.

Melt the butter in a heavy-based frying pan and sauté the scallops very quickly (they will not need more than 1 minute on each side) until golden. Be careful not to burn the butter, as this will dirty the scallops. Remove them from the pan and set aside.

Peel the Nashi pears, quarter them, then cut each quarter in half again lengthways. Add the pear slices to the pan you have used to fry the scallops and sauté them for a few minutes, until caramelized and golden on both sides.

Ladle the soup into large flat soup bowls and garnish with the scallops, pear slices and a long shard of crisp pancetta.

saffron and mussel soup with pastis and fennel

2 whole red mullet, gutted

120 ml/½ cup olive oil

1.5 kg/3 lb. 5 oz. mussels, cleaned and bearded

2 leeks (whites only), finely sliced

1 large strong onion, finely diced

1 fennel bulb, finely sliced

2 garlic cloves, chopped

2 red peppers, deseeded and finely sliced

a good pinch of saffron fronds

6 large ripe tomatoes, diced

2.5 litres/quarts fish or vegetable stock

2 bay leaves

a small bunch of fresh thyme

a small bunch of fresh parsley, plus extra, chopped, to garnish

2 large pieces of orange zest (pared with a potato peeler to avoid pith)

2–3 tablespoons tomato purée/paste

110 g/2¼ cups white breadcrumbs

75 ml/5 tablespoons Pastis (or Pernod)

sea salt and ground black pepper

for the rouille

6 garlic cloves, crushed

1 egg yolk

1–2 teaspoons cayenne pepper

150 ml/⅔ cup olive oil

serves 6

This is a wonderfully powerful soup, and worth the extra effort. The fennel and Pastis are authentically French and bring this soup to life. I feel like I am sitting in a harbour in Brittany when I eat it, with a glass of delicious dry white wine. You will, too...

Descale the red mullet and make sure it is cleaned well. Roughly chop the fish into large pieces, keeping the head and fins on.

Heat the oil in a large pan, toss in the mussels and place a lid firmly over the pan. Cook over high heat for 1 minute, then, holding the lid down firmly, shake the pan to toss the mussels. Cook for a further 2 minutes, then toss once more. Remove the lid and all the mussels should be open (discard any that haven't opened). Using a slotted spoon, remove the mussels from the pan, leaving the oil and any liquor from the mussels in the pan.

Add the leeks and onion to the pan and cook gently to soften without browning, then add the fennel, garlic, peppers, saffron and tomatoes. Cover with the stock and add the red mullet pieces, herbs and orange zest. Bring the liquid to a boil, then stir in the tomato purée/paste and the breadcrumbs. Reduce the heat and simmer the soup, uncovered, for about 15 minutes.

In the meantime, remove the mussels from their shells, leaving a few in the shells to garnish.

Set a fine-meshed sieve/strainer over another large pan and pass the soup through the sieve/strainer, pushing all the fish, breadcrumbs and vegetables through the mesh to get as much texture from the solids as possible. You will now have a fishy, slightly thick soup. (If you would like it to be smoother, blend briefly with a stick blender.) Season well with salt and pepper, then stir in the mussels, Pastis and freshly chopped parsley.

To make the rouille, put the garlic in a blender with the egg yolk and a pinch of salt and blend until smooth. Gradually add the oil, a trickle at a time, until it is all incorporated and a good thick cream is achieved. Add the cayenne pepper, to taste.

Serve the soup in large flat bowls, garnished with the reserved mussels in their shells, with the rouille and French crusty bread.

international flavours

beef goulash

Over the years, I have had people of many nationalities working for me in the Provender Soup kitchens. The Hungarians among them swear by their country cuisine, the classic of which is their goulash. Many impress on me their mother's traditional recipe, but this is my take on it, which is arguably as good as the authentic version from a countryman.

4 tablespoons olive oil

400 g/14 oz. lean beef, diced

3 red onions, finely sliced

3 garlic cloves, crushed

1 teaspoon smoked paprika

2 red peppers, deseeded and finely sliced

1 green pepper, deseeded and diced

250 g/9 oz. button mushrooms, sliced

200 g/1 cup white long-grain rice

4 generous tablespoons tomato purée/paste

a 400-g/14-oz. can chopped tomatoes

3 sprigs of fresh thyme

1.5 litres/6 cups beef or chicken stock

350 g/1½ cups sour cream

sea salt and ground black pepper

a large bunch of fresh parsley, chopped, to garnish

serves 6

Heat the oil in a large heavy-based saucepan set over high heat and brown the meat well. Reduce the heat, add the onions, garlic and paprika to the pan and cook very gently for about 20 minutes, until the onions are very soft. Add the red and green peppers and button mushrooms and cook for a further few minutes, until softened.

Stir in the rice and tomato purée/paste, followed by the chopped tomatoes and thyme, then add the stock. Bring the liquid to a simmer and cook gently until the beef is very tender and rice is swollen and soft – this will take about 40–50 minutes. Draw the pan off the heat and stir in the sour cream, then season well with salt and black pepper.

Ladle the soup into bowls and finish with plenty of the freshly chopped parsley to garnish before serving.

majorcan gazpacho

I studied Cordon Bleu at Eggleston Hall, a wonderfully traditional cookery school where we were taught to arrange flowers, type, sew, cook and get in and out of a sports car without showing our knickers – all in preparation to become a 'useful' wife. This is one of the dishes that reminds me so much of my time at Eggleston. Gazpacho is a brilliant Spanish soup and one of the very few the Brits have embraced as a chilled soup. I love serving this with a skewer of piquant prawns/shrimp in a shot glass as an appetizer before a BBQ on a summer's day. The soup should be served the colder the better.

12 very ripe tomatoes, peeled (see tip), deseeded and roughly diced

¾ cucumber, peeled and deseeded

2 red peppers, deseeded and diced

4 spring onions/scallions, whites only, sliced

1 red chilli, deseeded and diced

1 green chilli, deseeded and diced

3 garlic cloves, crushed

600 ml/2¼ cups thick tomato juice

1 tablespoon tomato purée/paste

1 slice of white bread, crusts removed, soaked in 1 tablespoon tarragon or white wine vinegar

150 ml/⅔ cup virgin olive oil, plus extra to drizzle

a pinch of celery salt

a dash of Tabasco

ground black pepper

reduced balsamic vinegar, to serve

finely diced red pepper, green pepper, cucumber, tomato and spring onion/scallion greens, to garnish

serves 6

Put all the vegetables, chillies, garlic, tomato juice, tomato purée/paste and bread in the jug/pitcher of a blender and whiz until smooth(ish). You may need to do this in batches depending on the size of your blender. Alternatively, you can put them in a large saucepan and blend using a stick blender. Gradually trickle in the olive oil while still blending – this will give a gloss and richness to the soup, and balance the acidity. Once all the oil has been incorporated, season the soup with celery salt, Tabasco and ground black pepper. Put in the fridge to chill.

Combine all the finely diced vegetables for the garnish in a small mixing bowl.

Once well chilled, ladle the soup into bowls and serve garnished with a spoonful of the diced vegetables, with any extra served in a bowl on the side. I like to drizzle over a little sweet balsamic reduction and virgin olive oil, to serve, too.

Tip: For an easy way to peel tomatoes, bring a pan of salted water to a simmer. With a sharp knife, cut a cross in the base of each tomato and put in the pan of hot water. Leave for 30–40 seconds (the time may vary depending on the ripeness of the tomato), then transfer to a bowl of cold water. The skin should now easily peel away at the point of the cross cut.

chicken paella soup with chorizo

This is a delicious take on the traditional Spanish paella. You can substitute the chicken with prawns/shrimp and mussels, if you wish. The chorizo gives it a rich smoky flavour, helped along by the smoked paprika. Add less liquid and serve it as a traditional paella, if you prefer, throwing in whatever colourful vegetables you have to hand.

1 chicken, jointed

3–4 tablespoons olive oil

a good pinch of smoked paprika, plus extra to sprinkle over the chicken

2 Spanish onions, diced

3 garlic cloves, crushed

280 g/1½ cups Arborio risotto rice

1 bay leaf

a pinch of saffron fronds

a good pinch of paprika, plus a little extra, to taste

a pinch of ground turmeric

100 ml/7 tablespoons white wine, plus an extra splash, to taste

1.3 litres/5½ cups chicken stock

100 g/3½ oz. chorizo, sliced

1 red pepper, deseeded and sliced

1 green pepper, deseeded and sliced

a squeeze of lemon juice

150 g/1 cup frozen peas

a large bunch of fresh parsley, chopped, plus extra to garnish

sea salt and ground black pepper

serves 6–8

Preheat the oven to 190ºC (375ºF) Gas 5.

Put the chicken joints in a roasting pan and lightly brush them with oil. Sprinkle with salt and smoked paprika, then roast in the preheated oven for about 30 minutes, until golden and the meat is tender and falling off the bones. Allow to cool, then remove the meat from the bones and set aside. (The skin adds flavour to soup, so add this, too, if you wish.)

Heat the remaining oil in a large saucepan, add the onions and garlic and cook until softened but not coloured. Add the rice and stir so that it is well glazed with the oil, then add the bay leaf and all the spices along with the white wine. Cook over gentle heat and, once all the wine has been absorbed, add the chorizo and red and green peppers. Begin adding the stock, a ladleful at a time, stirring all the time. Continue adding the stock, waiting until it has almost all been taken up by the rice before adding the next ladleful, until the rice is tender – this should take about 12 minutes. If the mixture is a little thick, add more liquid (either water or stock) to get it to a soup consistency. Once the desired consistency is achieved, lift the acidity with lemon juice and a splash more white wine, if wished, then season with salt and a good grind of freshly ground black pepper. Add the peas and parsley and cook for about 1 minute more. Taste and, if you like more heat, add a little more paprika.

Ladle the soup into bowls, garnish with a little more freshly chopped parsley and serve.

Tip: If you want to serve this dish as a classic paella rather than a soup version, do not add more liquid to the pan once the rice is cooked and tender.

sarsuela fish stew

This is wonderful Spanish stew with a rich, thick base, much like a lobster bisque. It's up to you if you want to leave the shells on the fish, which add to the flavour of the soup and make it more authentic. Alternatively, make eating easy and remove the shells first. But a mix of at least three types of fish and seafood is best. This is lovely served with rouille to richen the soup.

for the base

1 tablespoon olive oil

3 red onions, diced

grated zest of 1 orange

a pinch of saffron fronds

1 kg/2¼ lbs. rockfish (or other full-flavoured fish), gutted and scaled but head on

1 celery stick, sliced

4 carrots, peeled and diced

1 kg/2¼ lbs. fresh tomatoes, chopped

1 whole head of garlic, sliced in half

300 ml/1¼ cups medium to dry sherry

200 ml/¾ cup Pernod, Ricard or aniseed-flavoured liqueur

2 tablespoons tomato purée/paste

for the sarsuela

olive oil, for frying

500–600 g/1 lb. 2 oz.–1 lb. 5 oz. mixed fish and seafood, such as raw prawns/shrimp, lobster, langoustine, red mullet, squid, firm white fish (such as monkfish), clams, mussels (a mixture of at least 2–3 varieties is best), cleaned

2 red onions, finely sliced

2 fennel bulbs, finely sliced

a squeeze of lemon juice, to taste

sea salt and ground black pepper

freshly chopped parsley or chervil, to garnish

Rouille (page 110), to serve (optional)

serves 6

First make the soup base. Heat the oil in a large saucepan and fry the onions for a few minutes, until softened. Add the orange zest, saffron and rockfish and cook until the fish is browned all over. Add the celery, carrots, tomatoes and garlic, and cook, covered, over gentle heat for 20–30 minutes.

Draw the pan off the heat and add the sherry and Pernod. Very carefully, ignite the alcohol with a long kitchen match. Standing well back, shake the pan until the flames die down (this will happen when all the alcohol has burned off). Add the tomato purée/paste and 3 litres/quarts water. Bring the liquid to a simmer and allow to simmer for around 30 minutes.

Pass the soup base first through first a colander, then through a fine sieve/strainer. Allow the liquid to settle, then skim off any bits that are sitting on the surface. Set the stock aside until needed.

For the sarsuela, heat some oil in a large frying pan and fry all the fish and seafood (except clams, if using, as these will cook in the soup) in batches. The fish should not be cooked in the centre, just have had a little colour and have given up its protein juices. Remove the fish from the pan, add the red onions and fennel to the pan and sauté until just tender at the edges. Pour in the fish stock, bring to a simmer and leave to bubble away for 10–15 minutes. Lastly and just before you serve, add all the pre-cooked fish and the clams, if using, and simmer for 5 minutes. Season to taste with salt and pepper and lift the flavour with a squeeze of lemon juice.

Ladle the soup into bowls and serve with the Rouille, if using, and freshly chopped herbs.

avgolemono

This Mediterranean lemon soup is claimed by both the Greeks and the Italians. We use orzo pasta in ours, but you can use rice, if you prefer. The main element of this soup is the lemon, so choose the very best ones available. The egg adds a silky richness, which combines beautifully with the starch from the pasta and the acidity of the lemons. You must be careful not to heat the soup too much after adding the sabayon or it will curdle – keep it below a simmer at the end of cooking.

Heat the butter in a large saucepan, add the onion, garlic and celery and cook gently for a few minutes, until softened but not coloured. Add the stock to the pan and bring to a boil, then add the orzo pasta. Continue to simmer the soup for 12–15 minutes, until the pasta is tender.

While the pasta is cooking, make the sabayon. Put the egg yolks and lemon zest and juice in a heatproof mixing bowl set over a pan of simmering water. Whisk the eggs continuously over the heat, until fluffy – this should take about 6–7 minutes.

When the pasta has cooked, draw the pan off the heat and stir the cream into the stock mixture. Begin slowly adding the sabayon to the pan, a ladleful at a time, stirring continuously until all the sabayon is incorporated into the soup. Ladle the soup into bowls and serve.

Variation: If you would like to add chicken to the soup, stir 200 g/7 oz. chopped poached chicken into the soup right at the end. If you poach a whole bird, the liquid makes a great stock to use as the soup base.

100 g/7 tablespoons butter

1 white onion, diced

2 garlic cloves, crushed

2 celery sticks, sliced

2.8 litres/quarts chicken stock

200 g/1 cup orzo pasta or white long-grain rice

100 ml/6½ tablespoons double/heavy cream

sea salt and ground black pepper

for the sabayon

6 pasteurized egg yolks

grated zest of 1 large lemon and freshly squeezed juice of 2 large lemons

a large bunch of fresh parsley, chopped

serves 6–8

soupe au pistou

Pistou is a delicious garlic, basil and Parmesan sauce that is used to top and refresh this rustic staple of a soup. Soupe au pistou is commonly cooked in the south of France, where family recipes are preserved down the generations, and you can expect to find a hundred different versions in one village.

Heat the oil in a large saucepan and sweat the onions and leeks, without colouring, for about 4–5 minutes, until softened. Add the tomatoes, potatoes, carrots and butter/ lima beans. Cover the vegetables with the stock and pop in the bunch of thyme and the bay leaves. Season with a good amount of black pepper and a teaspoon of sea salt and bring the liquid to a boil. If any scum appears on the top, skim it off with a slotted spoon. Once boiling, add the vermicelli and simmer for about 8 minutes, until the pasta is cooked and the vegetables are tender. Add the French beans, courgettes/zucchini and lettuce to the pan just 2 minutes before the end of the cooking time so that they are softened but retain their colour.

To make the pistou, put all ingredients in a food processor and blend until smooth, then season to taste. Spoon the pistou into a small bowl.

Ladle the soup into bowls and serve with the pistou on the side for guests to dollop into the soup.

120 ml/½ cup olive oil

2 onions, sliced

2 leeks, sliced

8 tomatoes, deseeded and diced

2 small potatoes, peeled and diced

2 carrots, peeled and diced

a 400-g/14-oz. can butter/lima beans, drained

1.5 litres/6 cups chicken stock

a small bunch of fresh thyme, tied with string

2 bay leaves

110 g/4 oz. vermicelli or other small pasta

110 g/4 oz. French beans, cut into 2.5-cm/1-inch lengths

2 courgettes/zucchini, diced

1 small lettuce, roughly sliced

sea salt and ground black pepper

for the pistou

4 garlic cloves, chopped

a small bunch of fresh basil

150 g/1½ cups freshly grated Parmesan, or other hard cheese

3 tablespoons olive oil

serves 6

scottish root vegetable soup with pearl barley and thyme

This soup reminds me of the moors with my heart filled with love... It is best served in a mug while lying in the heather, watching the grouse and the world fly by. I wanted to create a traditional, really old-fashioned hearty soup, from all the good simple things – defiantly unsophisticated! There are two parts to the soup, first a base to suspend the other ingredients, then a simple throw it all in and simmer... very easy, very honest, totally delicious! If you have any left-over lamb from a roast, or just have a hankering for something more carnivorous, you can add lamb to the recipe – see the variation below.

100 g/7 tablespoons butter

1 small onion, diced

2 potatoes, peeled and diced

2 carrots, peeled and diced

800 ml/3⅓ cups vegetable stock

1 parsnip, peeled and diced

¼ celeriac/celery root, peeled and diced

¼ swede/rutabaga, peeled and diced

2 celery sticks, sliced

1 leek, finely sliced

90 g/½ cup pearl barley

a handful of fresh parsley, roughly chopped

a bunch of fresh thyme, leaves only

100 ml/7 tablespoons double/heavy cream

sea salt and ground black pepper

serves 6

Melt the butter in a large saucepan and add the onion, potatoes and half the diced carrots. Cook for a few minutes to soften, then pour in the stock. Put the lid on the pan and bring to a boil, then simmer for about 15–20 minutes, until all the vegetables are tender. Draw the pan off the heat and whiz with a stick blender until very smooth.

Add the remaining vegetables to the soup base along with the barley. Cover the pan and simmer for about 7–10 minutes, until the barley and vegetables are tender. The barley naturally thickens the liquid, so keep an eye on it and top up with a little water if the soup begins to get too thick, or it will not cook properly and may catch on the base of the pan.

Once the vegetables are tender, stir in the herbs and season well. This soup loves freshly ground black pepper, so make sure your pepper mill is full. Finally, and just before serving, stir in the cream to just give that added richness.

Ladle the soup into bowls or mugs and serve with crusty home-baked bread or a good soda bread.

Variation: For a meaty version, stir 250 g/9 oz. cooked pulled lamb into the soup when you add the herbs. Cook for a couple more minutes so that the lamb has a chance to heat through.

cape tribulation tom yum

Our good friends, Peter and Heather Kayes, used to run a little backpacker's rest at Cape Tribulation called The Jungle Lodge. It was way up in the rainforest where, in those days, only the most intrepid of travellers ventured. The dirt road was constantly being flooded, making it impassable, and it was this isolation, with no telephones or power or any kind, that made Cape Trib such a magical haven of escape. Peter would take us out to the reef in his fishing boat where we would snorkel and fish for tuna, coral trout and all manner of exotic sea creatures the like of which I had never imagined. Wonderful days, wonderful place and wonderful people. This Tom Yum was a very quick Thai-influenced soup that used the fish straight from the ocean, rustled up by Peter after a long day out on the reef.

2 litres/quarts fish or vegetable stock

4 tablespoons fish paste

1 onion, roughly diced

4 lemongrass stalks, bashed to release their flavour

6 fresh kaffir lime leaves

2–3 bird's eye chillies, finely sliced

1 kg/2¼ lbs. mixed fresh fish, prawns/shrimp or baby squid, cleaned, scaled and cut into nice chunks

4 spring onions/scallions, finely sliced

2 tablespoons freshly shaved coconut (optional)

2 heads of pak choi, sliced

6 tablespoons fish sauce

2 teaspoons mirin (Japanese rice wine) or ½ teaspoon soft brown sugar

freshly squeezed juice of 2 limes

a small bunch fresh coriander/cilantro, torn

serves 6

Pour the stock into a large saucepan and add the fish paste, onion, lemongrass stalks, lime leaves and 2 of the chillies. Bring the mixture to a simmer and cook for about 20 minutes. Pour the mixture through a sieve/strainer, discarding the solids.

Transfer the broth to a clean saucepan and bring to a simmer, then add the fish and seafood, spring onions/scallions and shaved coconut. Cook for 5–7 minutes, until the fish and seafood are just cooked, then add the pak choi. Season with the fish sauce and mirin. If you want a little more heat and colour, add another finely sliced chilli. Adjust the acidity with the fresh lime juice, adding a little at a time until you are happy with the flavour. Finally, stir in the torn coriander/cilantro.

Ladle the soup into bowls and serve immediately.

heavenly vegetable broth with chicken and kaffir lime

Oh my goodness, how can something this good for you taste so incredible? Almost fat free, fresh as a summer garden and as aromatic as having your nose in a lime tree! This is just the most heavenly little creation in the entire world, and has to be one of my best ever. If you like a little Asian influence, this one is for you!

1 tablespoon very light vegetable oil

4 chicken breasts, sliced into thin strips

8 spring onions/scallions, finely sliced and whites and greens separated

3 garlic cloves, crushed

2 green chillies, finely diced

2 lemongrass stalks, bashed to release their flavour

800 ml/3⅓ cups vegetable stock

6 fresh kaffir lime leaves

1 small leek, white only, finely sliced

8 celery sticks, finely sliced

2 fennel bulbs, finely sliced

1 courgette/zucchini, finely sliced

200 g/1½ cups fresh or frozen peas

200 g/1⅓ cups skinned baby broad/fava or edamame beans

grated zest and freshly squeezed juice of 1½ limes, or to taste

a handful of fresh parsley, roughly chopped

a small handful of fresh coriander/cilantro, roughly chopped

a small handful of fresh mint, roughly chopped

sea salt

serves 6

Pour the oil into a large saucepan, pop in the chicken breast while the oil is still cold and stir to coat well. There is very little oil, so a fine coating on the chicken before the heat takes hold will prevent it sticking to the pan, and breaking up. (We don't want that, as this soup needs to be almost a clear broth with every exquisite element holding its own.)

As the pan begins to take heat, add the spring onion/scallion whites, garlic, green chillies and lemongrass. Toss around the pan for a couple of minutes, until the chicken becomes white around the outside, then pour on the stock. Add the lime leaves, leek, celery and fennel. Cover the pan and cook over gentle heat for about 7–10 minutes, until the fennel becomes tender but not too soft. This soup needs to keep a little crunch.

At this point, remove the lime leaves and lemongrass if you feel their job is done, or leave them in if you want to make these flavours more pronounced.

Add the courgette/zucchini, peas and beans and cook for a further 3–5 minutes, until tender. Add the lime zest and half of the lime juice, taste, then add the rest of the juice if you feel it needs it, then season with a little salt. Once the flavour is pretty much where you want it, stir in the delicate fresh herbs.

Serve immediately in clean contemporary bowls, which emphasize the pure nature of the broth. Scatter with the sliced spring onion/scallion greens, to garnish. Heaven.

slow roast belly pork, noodles and shiitake mushrooms in sour broth

This is one of those soups that you know will taste good because it looks a bit intriguing: a clear broth of great flavours and textures. The crunch of the water chestnuts is a wonderful contrast to the slippery nature of the mushrooms. The mixture of rich, sweet, salty and sour is typical of Chinese food, and this soup demonstrates all these characteristics brilliantly.

a 400-g/14-oz. piece of belly pork

2 tablespoons vegetable oil

½ red onion, very finely sliced

a 2.5-cm/1-inch piece of fresh ginger, peeled and finely sliced into thin strips

150 g/5½ oz. shiitake or mixed exotic Chinese mushrooms

250 g/1 cup canned beef consommé

1.5 litres/6¼ cups chicken stock

200 g/7 oz. soba or other buckwheat noodles

2–3 green chillies, deseeded and finely sliced

4 spring onions/scallions, sliced on the angle and whites and greens separated

2 teaspoons sesame oil

2 tablespoons mirin (Japanese rice wine)

2 tablespoons soy sauce, plus extra to taste

3–4 tablespoons rice vinegar, plus extra to taste

150 g/5½ oz. canned water chestnuts, drained and sliced

2 heads of pak choi

a roasting pan, lightly oiled

serves 6–8

Preheat the oven to 220°C (425°F) Gas 7. Put the pork belly in the prepared roasting pan and roast for 30 minutes, then turn the temperature down to 180°C (350°F) Gas 4 and roast for a further 30 minutes. Pour off any fat, remove the crackling (and reserve for the garnish) and cut the meat into even slices. Set aside.

Heat the oil in a large saucepan, add the onion and ginger and toss over medium heat until softened. Add the mushrooms to the pan and stir to coat with the oil. Pour in the consommé and stock and bring the liquid to a simmer. Add the noodles, chillies, spring onion/scallion whites and pork slices, and simmer for 5–7 minutes, until the noodles are tender. Add the sesame oil, mirin, soy sauce, rice vinegar and water chestnuts. Adjust the seasoning by adding more soy sauce and vinegar. When happy with the balance of sweet, salt and sour, add the spring onion/scallion greens and the pak choi and cook for a further 2 minutes.

Serve in Chinese bowls, garnished with pieces of crackling.

creamy coconut and lamb soup with cumin, cardamom and almonds

When we were young, our only experience of curry was a thin lamb curry with raisins and 'curry powder'. My mum, brilliant at traditional English cooking, was not so good at authentic Indian! Needless to say, I was not a fan... until the sheltered girl from Yorkshire went to the big bad city and discovered Indian food was an absolute celebration of intriguing spices and flavours! This is a simple but delicious soup, wonderful with warm naan breads and raita.

4 tablespoons vegetable oil or ghee

2 onions, finely sliced

750 g–1 kg/1¾–2¼ lbs. lamb (leg, rump or shoulder), cut into bite-size pieces

2 garlic cloves, crushed

2 red chillies, deseeded and sliced

a 2.5-cm/1-inch piece of fresh ginger, peeled and grated

½ tablespoon ground cumin

1½ tablespoons garam masala

½ tablespoon ground coriander

about 1 teaspoon chilli powder

2 teaspoons ground turmeric

8 green cardamom pods

1 teaspoon ground cloves

1 litre/4 cups chicken or vegetable stock

a 400-ml/14-oz. can coconut milk

250 ml/1 cup passata (Italian sieved tomatoes)

200 g/1 cup red or green lentils

a squeeze of lemon juice

500 g/1 lb. baby spinach leaves

sea salt and ground black pepper

a handful of fresh coriander/cilantro, roughly chopped

100 g/1 cup flaked/slivered almonds, toasted

for the raita

a bunch of fresh mint leaves, finely chopped

200 g/¾ cup plain yogurt (sheeps' milk is best)

½ cucumber, grated

serves 6–8

Heat the oil in a large heavy-based saucepan and add the onions and lamb. Cook over medium–high heat until the lamb is sealed and turning an even brown. Add the garlic, chilli, ginger and all the dried spices and continue to cook over medium heat for a further few minutes, until the lamb has taken up all the spices.

Pour on the stock, coconut milk and passata, cover the pan and cook very gently for 40–50 minutes, until the lamb is almost tender. Stir in the lentils and continue cooking over low heat for a further 15 minutes, until the soup is thickened and the lentils are cooked. Season with salt and pepper, and add a little more chilli powder if you would like more heat. Finally, lift the flavour with a little lemon juice.

To make the raita, stir together the mint, yogurt and cucumber.

Just before serving, gently stir the baby spinach leaves into the soup, to wilt them, then ladle the piping hot soup into large soup plates. Scatter the coriander/cilantro leaves and the almonds over the bowls and serve with the raita on the side (or you can swirl a little into the soup, if preferred).

chicken tagine with prunes and toasted almonds

For 17 years I have run my catering company, and have met many fabulous chefs and good friends along the way. Ben South, a wandering star, is one such fellow. Travelling and eating are his life and Morocco is one of his favourite countries to travel by motorbike. This tagine is his, inspired by his travels, and you will love it!

2 tablespoons vegetable oil

1 onion, roughly diced

2 garlic cloves, crushed

1 red chilli, finely diced

a pinch of ground turmeric (or a 5-cm/ 2-inch piece of fresh turmeric)

a pinch of ground cinnamon

a pinch of ground cumin

1 aubergine/eggplant, diced

300 g/10½ oz. cooked chicken, cut into smallish cubes

a small handful of ready-to-eat prunes (or dried apricots if you prefer)

a 400-g/14-oz. can chopped tomatoes

800 ml/3⅓ cups vegetable stock

170 g/¾ cup drained canned chickpeas

freshly squeezed juice of about ½ lemon, to taste

2 tablespoons toasted flaked/slivered almonds

a handful of fresh coriander/cilantro, leaves torn

sea salt and ground black pepper

Raita (see page 134), to serve

serves 6-8

Heat the oil in a large saucepan and add the onion, garlic, chilli, spices and aubergine/eggplant to the pan. Toss over medium heat for a few minutes, until the onion is beginning to soften and the aubergine/eggplant is turning golden. The aubergine/eggplant will absorb all the oil and then release it again when cooked and ready. At this point, add the cooked chicken and prunes and cover with the chopped tomatoes and stock. Cover the pan and simmer for 15–20 minutes for the flavours to marry and the soup to thicken slightly. Add the chickpeas and cook for a further 10 minutes or so, then turn the heat right down and let the soup just tick away with the lid off for about 7–10 minutes. Allow the soup to reduce until nice and thick – you're looking for a lovely, almost stewy, consistency.

A little edge or 'cut' is needed in a tagine to balance with the sweetness of the prunes, so add the lemon juice to taste. Season to taste with salt and pepper.

Ladle the soup into bowls and scatter over the almonds and coriander/cilantro leaves to garnish. You could add a dollop of the raita to the soup, or serve it in bowls on the side for guests to help themselves. Extremely good indeed!

Variation: If you would like to make this tagine vegetarian, replace the chicken with sweet potato, squash, red and yellow peppers or any other colourful firm vegetables you like. Increase the amount of oil to 3 tablespoons and add the vegetables to the pan at the same time as the onion and aubergine/eggplant.

moroccan harira

This Moroccan stew is a lively mix of intriguing flavours. It is often made with lamb, which you may add to this if you wish; see the variation below. You can also substitute giant or normal couscous for the lentils, or do half lentils and half couscous, which gives an added visual interest. Mint and basil are also great with these flavours, so whatever herbs you have to hand or a mix of all will only make it better and better.

2–3 tablespoons olive oil

1 large onion, diced

2 garlic cloves, crushed

1 teaspoon ground turmeric

1 teaspoon ground cumin

1 teaspoon ground cinnamon

a 1-cm/½-inch piece of fresh ginger, peeled and grated

a generous pinch of saffron fronds

200 g/1 cup brown lentils or giant couscous

a 400-g/14-oz. can chickpeas, drained

2 x 400-g/14-oz. cans chopped tomatoes

700 ml/3 cups vegetable stock

a large bunch of fresh coriander/cilantro, chopped

a large bunch of fresh parsley, chopped

a squeeze of fresh lemon juice

sea salt and ground black pepper

serves 6

Put the oil, onion and garlic in a large saucepan along with the ground spices, ginger and saffron and sauté gently for a few minutes, until the onion is softened. Add the lentils and chickpeas and stir so that they are well coated with the spices. Pour in the chopped tomatoes and the stock and bring the liquid to a boil, then reduce the heat, cover the pan and simmer for 20 minutes, until the lentils are tender. Remove the pan from the heat and allow to cool slightly before stirring in the chopped fresh herbs. Season with salt and pepper and lift the flavour with lemon juice.

Ladle the soup into large bowls and serve.

Variation: If you want to make this a little more substantial, add 500 g/1 lb. cooked leftover lamb to the saucepan along with the lentils and chickpeas, and continue with the recipe as above.

spicy mexican chicken soup with red pepper and tortilla

I have used chicken in this delicious zingy soup, but really any white fish, beef or seafood would work just as well. This is surprisingly light and fresh rather than 'wholesome and warming'. If you don't like the thought of 'soggy' tortilla, serve them separately, but used here they are the 'carb' addition and actually work very well. This is pretty hot, so if you are of a feeble nature, reduce the chillies down to one of each colour.

2 tablespoons vegetable or corn oil

2 strong onions, finely diced

2 garlic cloves, finely chopped

2 red peppers, deseeded and diced

2 red pimento peppers, deseeded and diced

a pinch of ground cumin

4 boneless, skinless chicken breasts, cut into strips

2 green chillies, finely chopped

2 red chillies, finely chopped

4 big fresh tomatoes, peeled (see tip on page 117) and deseeded (if you can be bothered and for a more refined finish)

2 courgettes/zucchini, diced

2.5 litres/quarts chicken stock

1 tablespoon tomato purée/paste

sea salt and ground black pepper

for the garnish

6–8 corn tortillas, cut into thin strips

corn oil, for frying

1 ripe but firm avocado, peeled, stoned/pitted and diced

4 spring onions/scallions, greens only, sliced

a squeeze of fresh lime (optional)

serves 6–8

Heat the oil in a large saucepan, add the onions, garlic, peppers and cumin and cook over low–medium heat until the onions and peppers are softened. Raise the heat slightly and add the chicken strips and fresh chillies. When the chicken is white on the outside, add the tomatoes and courgette/zucchini and cover with the stock. Simmer gently for at least 15 minutes, until the chicken is cooked, but leaving it for up to 25 minutes will allow the flavours to develop. Stir in tomato purée/paste and season with salt and black pepper.

Fry the tortilla strips in a little corn oil until golden brown.

Ladle the soup into bowls and scatter over the crispy tortilla strips, a sprinkling of avocado cubes and the spring onion/scallion greens. If you like, add a little squeeze of fresh lime juice and serve.

index

acknowledgments

I would like to thank my parents for giving me such a blissful childhood, introducing me to good food and then allowing me to pursue my love of it...

My chefs Tom and Bens South and Moore for patiently trialling all the soups through our Kitchen at the Yorkshire Party Company, and the teams at both Yorkshire Provender and the Yorkshire Party Company for giving such support.

Finally, to my sons Joss, Louis and Ben for never getting sick of being guinea pigs, and to my husband Terry, without whom Yorkshire Provender would never have gotten beyond a cottage industry.